John Freeman

Where *ACTION* Is

Andy Anderson
with Eugene Skelton

Broadman Press / Nashville, Tennessee

4262-12
ISBN: 0-8054-6212-0

Scripture quotations marked TLB are from *The Living Bible, Paraphrased* (Wheaton: Tyndale House Publishers, 1971) and are used by permission.

Dewey Decimal Classification: 268.1
Subject Heading: ACTION
Library of Congress Catalog Card Number: 76-11988
Printed in the United States of America

Dedicated to
My Wife - Eleanor

With Special Appreciation for
Members of Riverside Baptist Church,
Fort Myers, Florida
Doctor Bob Anderson
Frank Land
Sanford Williams
"saints and faithful brethren"
(Colossians 1:1)

A WORD OF APPRECIATION
from Grady C. Cothen

ACTION is an idea whose time has come, and Andy Anderson is a man God has raised up for such a time as this. From time to time across the years, I have heard the brethren wish for something like "A Million More in Fifty-four" as a means of getting a new start in enrolling people in Bible study. Many of us felt that the new thrust should go beyond a single year, and that it should involve basic principles of growth that would endure.

When I came to the Baptist Sunday School Board in 1974, I was looking and praying for a "handle" to this problem. I felt that we must become involved as Southern Baptists in Bible study. I have long believed that this was an excellent way to begin the process of leading the lost to faith in Christ. Bible study is a most effective way to help the believer grow in the likeness of Christ.

On a visit to Florida in late 1974, someone asked what I thought of the ACTION plan. After confessing my ignorance, I received a short explanation which intrigued me. Dr. A. V. Washburn and I agreed that we should know more. The more we learned, the more interested we became. The plan is simple, practical, and effective. It aims at enlisting people in Bible study, relates them to a class and teacher. It magnifies the church. It encourages personal witnessing and ministry. It builds on what we have learned about the laws of Sunday School growth and development. It does not compromise or diminish the emphasis on good teaching or organization.

Most of all—this plan works. Where a church follows the basic plan and follows up on the new enrollees, membership in Sunday School and attendance grow dramatically. It provides a marvelous method of re-enrolling church members and others in Sunday School by use of the pastor's class. Yet the pastor tries to enlist those in his class in the regular organization. When properly used, the plan will not leave a bad impression and can be used again and again. This was "the handle" for which we were looking.

The man behind the idea is Andy Anderson. As a pastor he had hunted for a way to reach people. As he pioneered the development of the basic ideas, he found better ways of doing the old tasks. When we became interested in the concept, he was beginning to get requests for information and help from many places. We felt God had raised him up to do this job at this time. It seemed to us that his leadership at the Sunday School Board, in helping Southern Baptists reach many for Bible study, was essential.

We are pleased to present Andy Anderson and ACTION to the Southern Baptist Convention. We believe God has a great future in store for us as we work together in enlisting millions in Bible study.

A WORD OF APPRECIATION from A. V. Washburn

My first introduction to Andy Anderson came by way of a mimeographed bulletin that described some fantastic results in Sunday School enrollment gains. There was a brief description of what was involved in an enrollment plan labeled "ACTION." The bulletin excited my interest and led to a meeting with Andy personally. I met him; I heard him; I was convinced that Andy and ACTION had "come to the kingdom for such a time as this"!

The concept of "open enrollment" is scriptural and Baptistic. Southern Baptists had always had a plan of enrollment, but it was a permissive, rather than an aggressive, plan! Locating prospects and follow-up visitation were good, but lacked the direct, positive "sign-on-the-dotted-line" approach. ACTION calls for enrolling anyone, anywhere, anytime, if he is willing to enroll in Bible study. ACTION calls for and encourages positive decision. ACTION shows immediate results!

Hundreds of churches already have conducted successful ACTION campaigns. Many thousands of persons have been reached for Bible study, for Christ, and for church membership, and this is just the beginning! I believe using this plan in the spirit of Christian love and concern will bring multitudes of people to engage in meaningful Bible study and to experience a vital relationship with Jesus Christ.

But what of the man behind ACTION? I find it difficult to separate Andy from the plan. He is a man on mission helping churches with their foundational mission.

Five words characterize Andy Anderson—

Spirit. Andy is full of exuberant optimism. He accentuates the positive. He believes in his product and he is confident that it produces good results. And his spirit is contagious. Talk with him and you'll catch it!

Vision. Andy does not think in small terms. It is evident that he takes William Carey's motto seriously, "Attempt great things for God; expect great things from God." For a starter, a church can double in Sunday School enrollment—and then go on from there! Southern Baptists can have twice as many Sunday Schools, twice as many churches, twice as many baptisms, twice as many enrolled in Bible study. And this can become a reality in the next decade.

Simplicity. ACTION is a simple program. That is, it has a singleness of purpose and an uncomplicated structure. For Andy, simplicity does not mean shallowness; it means strength. Attention is directed to the basic elements—the indispensables. ACTION is kept to a single purpose–enrollment in Bible study. The ongoing Sunday School program of training adequate leadership, providing quality Bible teaching, and providing all the elements of the ongoing Sunday School program are absolutely essential to consolidate gains.

Commitment. Andy's commitment to his Lord, to the churches, and to the denomination is unquestioned. One small illustration. When the Sunday School Board secured the copyright to the *ACTION Manual,* by Andy's request the royalty on the sales of the manual goes to the Home Mission Board to purchase building sites for new churches.

Energy. It takes energy to maintain such a schedule of field services. Andy travels an average of 20,000 miles a month speaking at conventions, evangelism conferences, and conducting interpretation meetings and training sessions related to ACTION. I'm reminded of what a man said of Arthur Flake years ago, "He's a steam engine in britches!"

Contents

Introduction

Your Sunday School Has a Fantastic Future

I am about to do something in your own lifetime that you will have to see to believe (Habakkuk 1:4, TLB).

I predict a fantastic future for your Sunday School!

I predict more people enrolled in Bible study through Sunday Schools than we have ever dreamed of seeing. I predict the improvement of teaching in our Sunday Schools and the winning of vast numbers of people to Christ through the witness of Sunday School workers and class members. In saying this, I realize I am going counter to what many say, some of them Christian leaders and others religious educators. I still make my predictions.

Why? Because I believe we are going into an unequalled time of Sunday School growth, a day when every Sunday School can grow if its leaders sincerely desire its growth and if they are deeply concerned for the people it might be able to reach. For a number of years I have said this because I thought, first of all, that God would answer my earnest prayers and those of others like me who have asked over and over again for a time of Bible study growth. Then a rising spirit of concern on the part of our people everywhere has promised a sure result: reaching more people for Bible study. The renewed emphasis upon reaching people by our denomination, demonstrated in the *ReachOut* emphasis, was well received. The churches responded, and we did see growth.

The bus outreach program, springing to life first in the churches, but then promoted vigorously by the Sunday School Department of the Sunday School Board, demonstrated that the churches had an intense desire to reach people and would respond to any program with that in view, if there seemed any possibility it would reach people. The bus outreach program did contain that promise, and it did receive an enthusiastic response among the churches.

The exciting thing about the present is that we have God-given, Holy-Spirit-blessed tools with which to reach great numbers of people. These tools? First of all, there are our proven methods of Sunday School work, geared for reaching people and for teaching them effectively once they are reached for Bible study. These methods always have worked when we have worked them, and they still work. But now added to them we have a newly-developed plan for enrolling people in Bible study. It, too, is a plan that has been proven. And it is being proved many times over in our churches at the present.

This book is about that plan and about the man through whom God gave it to his people, E. S. (Andy) Anderson.

I first met Andy Anderson when he came to the Baptist Sunday School Board in the spring of 1975 to speak to the professional workers in the Sunday School Department. I was thrilled with his message, and I already knew much about ACTION. I had met the Sunday School enrollment idea some months earlier.

It was in Clio, Michigan. I had gone to Flint for a Sunday School Enlargement Campaign, and someone suggested I would profit by going to Clio and talking to the pastor, Robert Poage, about the work being done in the

First Baptist Church there. On that Sunday School afternoon I heard of ACTION for the first time. The church had an attendance of approximately 250 on that morning and enrolled more than that number during its week of ACTION enrollment. Not all that had been done by Sunday afternoon, but it was underway.

As the pastor explained to me what the church was doing, I knew immediately the Lord had given Southern Baptists a new and effective tool for reaching more people than ever before—reaching them first for Bible study and then for Christ and church membership. I rejoiced and resolved to know more about this method and to begin using it right away and in every possible place.

After I returned to Nashville I called the Riverside Baptist Church in Fort Myers, Florida. Andy himself was away, but when I explained that I wanted one of the ACTION manuals, the secretary immediately responded. My manual arrived within a few days, and I studied the program.

The more I understood, the better I liked what I saw. Here indeed was a Holy Spirit-inspired plan that would help any church reach more people. I vowed to use it as often as any door of opportunity opened.

When I met the one whom God used to develop the plan, E. S. (Andy) Anderson, I understood even more. He wanted more than anything else to see more people introduced to Bible study so our churches could reach more unsaved people for Christ. But beyond that, his life itself was an inspiration of encouragement and expectation. A buoyant faith and a happy spirit immediately communicated themselves.

This book tells something of the plan, but it tells more

of the spirit of the man. In it you'll find encouragement to overcome, not only your own need for building a larger and stronger Bible teaching program, but for meeting many of the problems of your personal life. The same principles he used to develop his plan for a better Sunday School may be applied to the building of a better life.

But the book shares more: it tells you that your church can grow now.

Like the McDowell Road Baptist Church of Jackson, Mississippi. This church, where John Hilbun is pastor, on one Sunday afternoon enrolled 118 new people in its Bible teaching program, more people than the church had enrolled the entire previous year.

And like the First Southern Baptist Church of Dover, Delaware, where Charles Adams is pastor. On the opening Sunday of a week of ACTION enrollment, this church had 225 in Sunday School attendance. For as many as a dozen years, attendance had hovered in the area of just over 200; from time to time some loss occurred, and then the church gained back the loss it had experienced. During the enrollment week the church experienced real growth with more than 150 new people added to the Sunday School.

Or Second Baptist Church of West Frankfort, Illinois. Ron Whitt is minister of education and Bruce McNeeley is pastor of this church. "We had an enrollment of 419 and an attendance of 241," says Whitt. "Ernie Adams led us in the week of our enrollment campaign. We showed an enrollment increase of 107. This increase lifted our attendance to 303. We later increased our enrollment to 589 and began working on a larger goal of 650."

Or Summer Grove Baptist Church, Shreveport, Louisiana (Billy Crosby, pastor), which reported 566 enrolled in one week and an attendance increase from 725 to 834.

Or the Conowingo Baptist Church, Conowingo, Maryland, which increased enrollment from 517 to 769. Attendance jumped from 310 to 427.

We are entering a new day of reaching people in our churches. They can be reached for Bible study, and through building the Bible study program great churches can be built. Today there is no reason for any pastor not to believe that his church can be stronger than it ever has been. *Your church can grow now.* It may not become the largest church in the country, for only a few can do that. Southern Baptists are a people of small churches, as well as large ones. But your church can become larger and stronger than it now is. This book will help you to see that this can be done.

In everything you do, put God first, and he will direct you and crown your efforts with success (Prov. 3:6, TLB).

Have you ever thought you'd reached the end of the way, and there was absolutely no possibility you could go ahead? Have you ever been so afraid of the risks involved in taking some new action that you simply did nothing? Perhaps because of lack of decision? Because you just couldn't move yourself to action? Have you ever looked at your own inabilities and decided there was no use trying? Then this book is for you.

It may seem to be the story of the ACTION Sunday School enrollment plan, how it developed, and what it can do for a church. It's more than that. In fact, that's not really what this book is about at all. The ACTION plan illustrates the real truths of the book.

YOU CAN DO ANYTHING GOD WANTS YOU TO DO AND YOU THINK YOU CAN DO FOR HIM!

EUGENE SKELTON
Nashville, Tennessee

1.
Begin With Concern and Commitment

Napoleon Hill of *Think and Grow Rich* fame identified a burning desire as the starting point of all achievement. To illustrate he told the story of the great merchant, Marshall Field, who stood on State Street, Chicago, along with a group of other merchants, on the morning after the great fire. Every man's business house was in ashes, and they were debating whether to stay in the destroyed city or go somewhere else to begin anew. All the others chose to leave, but not Field. He pointed a finger to the heap of smoldering ruins where his store had stood the day before. "Gentlemen, on that very spot I will build the world's greatest store, no matter how many times it may burn down," he said. Field did what he promised, Hill says in his book, because of a burning desire to achieve. A church and a church leader likewise must have a burning desire—and that desire must be to reach people for Christ.

For a church and its leaders everything needs to begin with concern for people and a commitment to reach them for Christ. That's how it all began with me and the church I served for so many years.

No one could be more amazed than I at what happened to Andy Anderson and the Riverside Baptist Church of Fort Myers, Florida. Even more fantastic is the ever-widening influence of the church and the events that happened within and through its fellowship. Every week seems to bring new and amazing stories of what God can do with and through his people.

Of course, all of it came from God. The work is his, and the glory is his. But if I were to answer the question how it came about, humanly speaking, I would say positively and with no hesitation whatsoever: it grew out of concern and commitment.

It grew out of my own concern for my church and for the unreached people of my community. I was also concerned for myself and for my ministry, but that came from my first and greater concern for the church and for unreached people. That was matched by the church; the Riverside Church had a compelling concern for the people all around us who needed Christ. It was concerned for its own spiritual life, the life of the church, but more for those we needed to reach. As we seemed to stand still, our concern grew deeper.

To tell you of myself and my years at Riverside is to recount how that concern and commitment came to be the dominating motivation of my life and how God used me to create a similar care in the church.

I was born in Cheraw, South Carolina, June 5, 1927, the fifth of seven children. I grew up learning of the Lord at the knees of a godly mother who led each of her children to accept Christ as soon as they were old enough to know right from wrong. Mother taught a Bible class in her home each week, and I was one of the first children to enroll in that class. Daily devotions were also a part of every day in our home. I suppose if there ever were a saint, my mother was one. After she died I was led to preach a sermon entitled, "The Death of a Saint." Many hearts were moved by that message, and later I printed the sermon. It has been read by people all over the world. Many have been brought to the Lord Jesus through the memory of that dear one of God.

Before I was six years of age, she taught me to memorize and quote more than 200 verses of Scripture. I could even give the "citation"–name the book, chapter, and verse number for each.

The night I was converted at age eleven, in a revival meeting, someone led me into the prayer tent following the invitation. While there on my knees, I suddenly felt an arm around my shoulder. It was my mother. Instead of attending the service that night she had spent the whole hour in prayer. She knew that she had a son–me–in the service, and she knew that son was unsaved. There in the prayer tent she spent an hour interceding, asking God for the salvation of her "little boy." God really spoke to my heart that night. Afterwards I was baptized in the First Baptist Church of our hometown.

During my senior year in high school, after winning letters in football, baseball, and track, I received a back injury which God used to change the course of my life. Up until this time, the Boston Red Sox had been considering me as a pitcher of promise. The back injury took place on the football field and ended my thoughts of a pro baseball career. At that point God revealed to me I was to spend my life altogether in another work. I surrendered my life to the gospel ministry and began my preparation.

After graduating from Atlanta Bible College, Atlanta,

Georgia, in 1947, I served my first pastorate, a rural church near West Bainbridge, Georgia. Then another in Meigs, Georgia. Between these two I was the associational missionary for the Bowen Baptist Association in Georgia. I then went to the First Baptist Church in Wildwood, Florida. I served in each of these places about three years. God was with me in a very unusual way in each of the pastorates; the membership more than doubled while I was there. To God be the glory.

In 1956 the pulpit committee from Riverside Baptist Church, Fort Myers, visited me and invited me to come before the church. The work at Wildwood was doing well, and I told the committee I was not interested in moving to another church.

The committee was insistent, finally persuading me to visit and speak at Riverside on a Sunday evening. The entire experience proved to be completely miserable. Mosquitos pestered me something unbelievable. Nothing seemed to go right. The next morning, Monday, I vowed never to come back to the place again. Before leaving town I shared my feeling with my wife, Eleanor. "Honey, look this place over real good. This is the last time you'll ever see it," I said. I had made a hasty decision. The church asked me to pray about the matter, and for the next seven days my wife and I totally gave ourselves to prayer. The result was that God completely turned us around. We accepted the call to come to Riverside.

During the following nineteen years the church grew and prospered under the guidance of the Spirit of God. The resident membership was 599 when I arrived on the field and continued upward to reach approximately 2,000. Average Sunday School attendance increased from 225 to more than 900, with growth continuing. The annual budget in 1956 was about $25,000, but in 1975 had gone above the $200,000 mark. The church owns a radio station and broadcasts an eighteen hour-a-day all Christian program. For sixteen years the church also has produced its morning worship service live on television, over WINK-TV, the local television station. During my pastorate I had also the privilege of baptizing more than 2,000 people.

"To God the glory," I say once more. I'm thankful he placed me in a position of leadership where great opportunity was present and then empowered my life so his work could be done through me.

The series of events during those years of my pastorate at Riverside were like climbing steps, steps drawing me closer to the Lord. One of these involved a serious automobile accident. As I returned from a mission church meeting with three deacons, about 11 o'clock one night a tractor-trailer ran into our car from the rear. It seemed to climb into the back seat where I was seated. My right shoulder was crushed totally; my right leg also was smashed from the hip to the knee. Doctors told me I probably never would be able to use the arm again, but I would be able to walk. This accident kept me in the hospital for the larger part of two years. During that time I could do nothing but pray and study my Bible.

In the midst of the pain and suffering, I came to realize I needed to take stock of my life. I came to see that up until that time there had been a whole lot of Andy but very little of the Holy Spirit. This needed to be reversed, I realized. Further, I knew the Holy Spirit must have a greater place in my ministry if I were to go on. Recovery from the accident was so complete that today

I use my right arm with ease and walk without a limp.

During the period of convalescence several things happened. First, I had an opportunity to write a book which I felt was seriously needed. Throughout my early ministry, many times after I would use a Greek term in a lesson or sermon, someone would mention they would love to be able to study the Greek. I realized that there was no home study method for this beautiful, useful language, and therefore, I set out to produce for home study a beginner's manual for New Testament Greek. My wife would place a portable typewriter on a small table across the bed, near enough for me to work. Across the weeks the work took form. Later, I published the manual. It has been and is being used all over the United States. Many lovers of the New Testament denied college or seminary training have used the book with profit.

I have hundreds of testimonies from lay people, pastors, and educators who thank me for the work. Two Bible schools use it in their extension program.

However, something even greater came from this experience: a realization that I could not build a fruitful ministry on fleshly activities, that if I ever were to succeed in building the spiritual church which God desired, I must work through prayer. In reading Philippians 1:3-11, I discovered that Paul grew a church by praying for its members. The most used book in my study–after my Bible–became the looseleaf church roll book. I began to pray diligently for my membership name by name. During the period of my convalescence I spent one to two hours in devotional life each day, not in sermon preparation, but in Bible study for personal growth and in prayer, praying especially for the members of my church.

This became the fixed habit of my life: study and prayer each day. First I prayed for myself. I had to get "old Andy" straightened out before I could pray for others.

From that point I took the list of church members and read them slowly, praying for each individual. In doing this, some ten or twenty families each day received special prayer attention. To each of these I wrote in long hand a personal note on a card entitled, "From the Pastor's Altar." It reads something like this: "Joe, I prayed for you and your family at four minutes past 10:00 this morning." I addressed these cards myself. At the top of each card I wrote the date and the exact time I prayed for the person or family. These struck a responsive note in the lives of many of my people, and though there were times when I could not be with them, they knew that I was with them in prayer.

During my convalescence God led the church. It did not go backward but continued to increase in size and spirit. The people of the church took places of responsibility for outreach and the entire ministry of their church.

Shortly after I returned to the pulpit, something unusual happened. Our church grew stagnant. We did not grow—in fact, seemed unable to grow. At the time I did not understand what was taking place or why. But lack of growth was decidedly unusual for Riverside church. How should I respond to the situation?

I could have explained that one or more of three reasons would account for our lack of growth. First, I could have said: "Now listen, folks, the entire Southern Baptist Convention is suffering a decline, and we want to cooperate, so as a result we are declining with them." But of course that wasn't true.

Second, I could have said: "Friends, the conditions in America are not conducive to church growth. We have just come through the Korean conflict and we are now in the Vietnam conflict; there is rioting and strikes and widespread unrest within our nation, and people are not interested in the church growth." But I could not say that when, in my heart, I knew that there was no outside influence that could stop the growth of the church of Jesus Christ.

So I had to take the third possibility. "We have sinned," I said to my people. "I do not know where the sin is, but the only thing that can stop the church of Jesus is sin within the camp." As soon as we admitted this, God was able to come and do a work of grace within us. I suppose this could be compared to the unsaved person. God cannot save him until he has been willing to admit his wrong–that he is a sinner. And so when our people faced up to the fact that we needed to get closer to God, God was able. He took charge and began to open our eyes and help us see what he could do if we would only give him a chance.

When I tell you something of Fort Myers you'll understand why the church's failure to grow was a reason for deep concern. Located on the southwest coast of Florida on the Tamiami Trail and midway between Tampa and Miami, it is a beautiful little city–in fact, one of the most beautiful to be found anywhere. Magnificent royal palms line its streets, many of them set out under the direction of Thomas Edison, one of its many famous citizens.

Fort Myers was Edison's winter home and laboratory. It is now the home of a special Thomas Edison museum, as well as a gorgeous botanical garden established by the great inventor. Among other outstanding men who made the city one of their homes were Harvey Firestone and Henry Ford.

Within the city itself there are about 30,000 residents, but the population of the greater Fort Myers area is 50,000 or slightly more. But it is growing rapidly. At the time our church ceased to grow, the area was gaining about 1,200 new citizens each month. Even in our greatest years of growth, the church had reached no more than one-twelfth of the people moving into the city. What about those people now that the church had stagnated?

Were other churches reaching those people? We were blessed with churches, some of the finest Southern Baptist churches in the nation. We also had aggressive churches of other denominations. Almost every denomination had a church in Fort Myers. Several of these churches were growing rapidly, yet all of us together were not reaching the majority of the citizens. They could not know what God charged Riverside to do.

My concern over our church's lack of growth amid an ever-growing mass of people unreached for Bible study and for Christ became increasingly serious in my life. I suppose I knew intellectually the part that concern must play in the turnaround of a church or an individual, but I needed to know this experientially. By this time, I made a personal survey of our community by calling the pastors of the churches. In this very unofficial survey I discovered that about 100,000 people living in our county were not in Sunday School or Bible study of any kind on any given Sunday. I took this fact to our church. We studied that statistic in the light of needed growth, and initiated a program called "Win Lee County–Now!"

Our people began to share my concern. In our mid-week prayer services and in other prayer meetings we prayed about this matter. We were not winning the county, our mission field. We needed to change directions and dimensions. There was a crisis. We knew something had to be done that was greater than what we were doing. So, we trusted the Lord to show us the direction in which we should go. Some of our people fasted. Most of our people prayed. This was the time of crisis, a time when we had to admit we were going to do the work God called us to do, or we would sit down and have business as usual. But we knew that business as usual is usually bad business, at least not the best business. Out of this concern, ACTION was born. God gave it to us through the leadership of The Holy Spirit, but our concern softened our hearts and tuned our spiritual ears.

I am convinced that church growth begins with *concern* and *commitment.* Every ACTION campaign I know of has begun this way. A pastor becomes concerned for his church and for unreached people. In some cases concern for his own ministry may have motivated this; but above all, it has been a concern for reaching people.

Soon after our church began growing, I received my first call to help someone else. A young pastor in a neighboring town contacted me. This pastor, Jay Strack, not long saved and only eighteen years of age, was interested in preaching, because God had called him. Jay already had been ordained but did not know how to organize the work of a church. He knew how to win people to the Lord Jesus, but he wanted to establish them in a Bible study program.

In response to his request, I gave him the best help

I could. We set up an organization and made plans for an ACTION program. At the beginning of the ACTION program, the church had 122 enrolled in its Sunday School. In one week enrollment grew to 272–the church experienced a net increase of exactly 150. This was not a strong church. It had only a few faithful workers, but these acted out of their concern and compassion for the people of Immokalee, Florida. As a result, this numerically small church baptized one of the largest numbers in the state of Florida. The concern of a pastor brought me to his church, and they achieved this result.

Shortly thereafter, Rev. M. D. Durrance, pastor of the First Baptist Church, Arcadia, Florida, invited me to come and conduct a revival in his church. Familiarly called "Tiny" by all who know him, he is a man with a heart as big as the world. His concern for lost people has inspired many who know him. I asked for the privilege of conducting an ACTION revival. We would have an ACTION Sunday School enrollment program and a revival during the same week. He agreed, and together we led his church in an exciting week. God came in unusual power and visited with us. The Sunday School enrollment grew during that week from 689 to 1,014, a 325 increase. An unusually large number of people were saved that week. But more important, people caught a new vision of what they can do when concern and compassion pave the way.

Shortly thereafter, Travis Hudson, pastor of the New Hope Baptist Church in Wauchula, Florida, asked me to come and share with him. My, what a marvelous week we had. This rural church, led by a man with concern for the people of his community, gained in Sunday School enrollment from 210 to 375, an increase of 165. Since then the church has continued to grow. In fact, they outgrew all of their facilities and were compelled to cease enrolling people in Sunday School until they could complete a new educational building!

These three pastors, along with many others, have seen fantastic growth take place in their churches, but it all began with concern and compassion on the part of someone. Concern produces commitment. Jesus looked over the sleeping Jerusalem and wept. In almost the same hour he again committed himself to the cross. Along with commitment may come a dream of what God may do with you and your church.

In those days I dreamed a great deal when I saw my community growing so rapidly, filled with people without Jesus Christ. I dreamed of the ability, under God's leadership, to reach every reachable person. It was then that God was able to move in my heart and lead me in the way.

2.
Use Your Frustrations

To turn commitment into action is no easy matter. Nor can it be done suddenly. Trying may—yes, almost always does—produce frustrations of various kinds. At least it did in my case. But I'm glad I didn't throw away my ticket when the train went into the tunnel, because we came out.

Here are some reasons why I experienced frustration. You may recognize some of them.

Lack of knowledge. With study course awards dating back to 1947, I thought I knew everything about Sunday School growth. But I didn't. My sense of frustration grew.

Failure. The things I tried failed. When the church I pastored ceased to grow after I had served it for sixteen years, I had my first unaccustomed taste of failure. There was to be more, however. I began trying to find ways to move ahead and failed again. My string of failures became quite impressive and each attempt at something new made it grow even longer. Only those who try, succeed, but only those who try, fail, also. Well, one could fail by default. I determined not to do that; believing the church should go forward and not backward, I tried again. Still another failure. And frustration mounted.

The trust of the people. I was their leader; they

thought I could do anything. I'm afraid some of them considered me some sort of ecclesiastical locomotive able to huff and puff and pull the whole bunch through to glory. I wanted to be equal to their confidence and live up to their expectations, but seemed unable to do so. Still more frustration.

Lack of concern on the part of some. "We've got a good church," they said. "Why worry? We're doing better than most." But that was no good. Mack Douglas expressed well the fault of that attitude in his book, *How to Build an Evangelistic Church.* "A church is like an army," he said. "When an army loses its spirit of conquest, mutiny follows and when a church loses its spirit of conquest, disunity follows." I saw where lack of concern could lead. But what could I do?

I faced several possibilities. For one thing, I could give up and settle into an easy life-style for myself and the church. "Status quo in seventy fo' don't bother me no mo'," I could say.

Or I could give up and move. Good churches were seeking pastors, and surely one would call me. Yet, I knew God had not called me to another pastorate. I could just leave the church. I went so far in my frustration as to talk with the deacons about the possibility of resigning. Maybe a "new broom could sweep clean." I'm glad they didn't accept this proposition, for I knew in my heart my work was to continue in Fort Myers.

I knew my frustrations were using energy–I didn't know what else they might be doing to me. I knew that oftentimes they produce ulcers or bring on heart attacks, and I didn't want either of these. My frustrations continued to build up anxious energy and I had to expend it somehow.

I turned to gimmicks. In fact, I got to the point I would go by the book store and look for a new book on some new promotional scheme. I would put these on—yet, on Sunday night go back home to my bedroom and weep, for I didn't see the success that needed to be found in our church.

I felt drained and trapped. Completely exhausted. Almost ready to quit, yet still knowing I could never accept that way out. So, I gave myself to fasting and prayer. That's right—to fasting along with my prayer. I went to my knees and laid my frustrations before Jesus. I encouraged the people of the church to join me in the same things, fasting and praying. They did just as I asked. They, too, were concerned. Jesus answered through the touch of his Holy Spirit. I read again and again his promise of the Comforter, the Christian's helper. With the Spirit's help, I discovered I could channel my energy into hard work and into a continuing search for God's way for our church to reach people for Bible study. Even though I didn't have all the answers immediately, I had an assurance the Holy Spirit's guidance would continue.

Let's go back to the title of this chapter for a moment. "Use Your Frustrations." Too often they use us, but the Holy Spirit can help us use them so the energy they impound is turned into a creative force almost unbeatable and unstoppable. That's what happened to me. God's Holy Spirit planted the ACTION idea in my heart.

Austin Tucker is pastor of the University Baptist Church, Lake Charles, Louisiana. His church is located in the area of McNeese State University where about 3,000 students are enrolled. He was burdened—yes, frustrated—over the fact that the church had enrolled *only four* of these thousands in Bible study. What could he do? Find excuses to explain away his failure? Ignore the challenge? Give up? He did none of these. But his concern turned into frustration. There his frustration sparked his creativity. He would lead his church to visit the dormitories to enroll students where they were. Right away his workers enrolled forty new students. Now the church serves lunch for its college department at the close of each morning worship service. Out of this pastor's frustration came greater victories than he otherwise could have experienced. God will do the same for you.

Mert Rice, longtime pastor of the Woodward Avenue Christian Church of Detroit, had a sermon on the theme, "A Discontented Optimist." The title says in a sense what happened to me. I believed God wanted to give a blessing, and I believed the Riverside Baptist Church had a great present and a greater future. The present was what bothered me; I couldn't find the way to move from present discouragement into the glorious future the Lord Jesus wanted to give us. Had I become contented, the future never would have come. The buildup of discontent into frustration created the driving power God used to force me to find a way. If you're frustrated, don't give up. Let your frustrations spark your creativity. You may be a genius when driven to it.

3.
Major on the Key Factor

Jesus told a story of the land owner who gave close supervision to all the fruit-bearing trees on his properties. A tree failed to bear fruit, not one time but for several succeeding years. At last the Master decided the tree was useless. "Cut it down," he said to his gardener. "Why should it cumber the ground if it gives us no fruit?" The question was purely rhetorical; the master had made his decision already.

But the gardener cared for the tree—perhaps he loved all of his trees. "Let me dig about it one more year," he asked. "I will feed the root system with fertilizer and nutrients. The tree may do better."

The Master consented. He agreed with his gardener that the secret of fruitage lay in the strength of the roots. If these could be given new life and growth, the tree itself might blossom and in due time put forth fruit.

During my period of fasting and prayer in the fall of 1972, the Holy Spirit planted an idea in my mind: like the gardener of the story, Jesus cares for you and for the people you lead. Let him dig about your tree—he'll give you still another chance to develop the kind of church he wants and needs. If you desire to develop his kind of church, start with the root system.

And what is the root system of the church? The Sunday School. Of couse, I knew that. As soon as the Holy Spirit gave me this new insight, I knew it. The Sunday School is the best source of prospects for evangelism, and the Bible teaching which takes place in the Sunday School is the best preparation a person can receive for hearing and accepting the gospel proclamation. In fact, through excellent Bible study the unsaved may be introduced to Christ as Savior.

The Sunday School is also the best means the church possesses of teaching stewardship, including the stewardship of life, as well as the principle of the tithe. The Sunday School offers areas of service to all who will serve, while at the same time providing a ground for calling out and developing still additional workers. I remembered the title of a classic on Sunday School work, *The True Functions of the Sunday School.* In this helpful book, the writer, Arthur Flake, pointed out these avenues and many others in which the Sunday School was and is exactly what I perceived it to be: the root system of the kind of church Jesus wants and needs.

I continued my analogy, applying it more closely to the Sunday School itself. What is the root system of the Sunday School? My conclusion? New enrollment: To put the matter differently, the key factor in growth–growth in attendance specifically, but in all other areas of growth as well–is enrollment. For the first time in my twenty-nine-year ministry, I understood the positive relationship between "inrollment" and enrollment. I decided to major on this key factor: *enrolling* more people in my Bible study program.

Examining my Sunday School records closely in the light of the kind of programs I had pursued, I made some significant discoveries. Soon these fell into place in what I call the three laws of Sunday School attendance. I call them laws because they operate, whether or not we want them to be true and whether or not we want them to control our work. Although we may deny them or scoff at them, they still govern what happens in our Sunday Schools as far as attendance is concerned. They controlled attendance at Riverside, even when I was unconscious of them. They worked even when I didn't know they were working. My discovery of these laws gave me an understanding of how my Bible-teaching program could increase attendance.

These do not replace the "Laws of Sunday School Growth" developed in 1952-54 by J. N. Barnette and the staff of The Sunday School Department, Baptist Sunday School Board. Far from it. These "Laws of Attendance" extend and clarify our understanding of the earlier laws and application of them.

While those laws, to describe them generally, address themselves to increased enrollment upon the implicit assumption that attendance will follow enrollment, the newer laws of attendance begin with attendance and describe relationships which usually exist between attendance and enrollment. As with the earlier ones, they are not laws passed by edict of a pastor or Sunday School workers or church—they are principles discovered by observation of what happens in Sunday Schools. They operate in every church whether the pastor and his corps of workers and leaders recognize them or refuse to acknowledge them. They are working in your church now.

What are these laws?

1. *Enrollment includes both attenders and non-attenders.*

On any given Sunday your Sunday School and mine has enrolled persons present and enrolled persons absent. This is true of every Sunday School that maintains a roll or list of persons who "belong," who are members. I knew that I never would have in average attendance 100 percent of my Sunday School enrollment. On the other hand, I never would have zero percent. Someone would always forget and come. So, I had an average attendance. I examined that average attendance and asked myself a question or two.

What is our percentage of attendance?

At that time it was 43 percent of the enrollment present. I wondered whether the attendance level always had been the same. Upon study I found it had varied up or down from time to time. The actual percentage at a given moment reflected various factors, such as emphases being made and the current spiritual condition of the church as a whole, but the level to which we could rise seemed to be about 52 percent and the level to which we could fall was about 40 percent.

How did that compare with other Southern Baptist churches? By checking the minutes of several associations, our state convention, and statistical reports of the Convention, I found we compared favorably. Almost on dead center with everyone else, to be more exact. Our denomination, as a whole, for a number of years had shown an overall average of 52 percent of enrollment in attendance. Individual churches fluctuated from a low of 43 or 44 percent; some reached a high of 60 to 62 percent.

The truth became real to me: on my rolls every Sunday were both those present and those absent. About 50 percent would be present, and about 50 percent would be absent. I did not know then—neither do I now know—why that is the percentage. But it is. After the study, I did realize I never would have much more than 50 percent of my enrollment present; I also knew that with hard work and excellent Bible teaching we could reach an attendance level of 50 percent of our enrollment. That percentage of as many as I could enroll? I thought so.

2. *Attendance increases as enrollment increases.*

If the average attendance level could be brought up to approximately 50 percent of enrollment, no matter what the enrollment might be, would not increased enrollment mean increased attendance? The answer, I thought, should be "yes." As I worked, I found this to be true.

I illustrate this with an equation. Call it a people-reaching equation. It goes like this.

$$E = p + a$$

E represents enrollment; you see this immediately. Also you quickly recognize that p represents those present and a, those absent. We've already learned that p and a have a constant relationship, and that usually they equal each other. For instance:

1000 E (Enrollment) = 500 p (present) + 500 a (*a*bsent)

P and a are constant in relationship to each other. How can I increase their numerical value? I have only one way. Increase the numerical value of *E!* I raise my E from 1,000 to 2,000. Now my equation becomes:

2000 E (*E*nrollment) =
1000 *p* (present) + 1000 *a* (*a*bsent)

In simple words, this means increased enrollment results in increased attendance, usually in about the same percentages the Sunday School already maintains between those present and those absent.

3. *Decreased enrollment results in decreased attendance.*

This law might be called the law relating to the removal of names from the Sunday School roll. In fact, I have called it by that name.

It recognizes and states that as far as attendance is concerned, the number of those absent is just as important as the number of those present. This may seem a harsh way to look at it; it may seem almost "unspiritual." But it is still true. We have a tendency to want to remove from our Sunday School rolls the names of all those who do not attend. What is the result of this practice? Let's see.

If we have 1,000 enrolled, 500 in average attendance, this leaves 500 people who do not attend. Now, we are in the process of trying to remove the names of those who don't come. If we are successful in erasing the names of the 500 nonattenders, this would leave us then with 500 people enrolled and 500 people in attendance. That would be a remarkable achievement, wouldn't it? But law number one says that cannot be. There is no way we can have 100 percent of our enrollment in average attendance. The law says that somewhere in the neighborhood of 50 percent will be in average attendance. So, if the law is accurate, given a period of time, there will be 500 enrolled and only about 250 in average attendance.

I know there are exceptions to these rules, but by and large they govern the Sunday Schools of not only Southern Baptists, but practically every other denomination in the world.

These laws must be recognized, and I thank God that, once I saw them for the first time, I began to look at my church and study it in the light of the three. As long as we had emphases for enrollment in Sunday School, we had an increase in attendance, because a certain percentage of the people we enrolled attended. But when we became slack and began removing names without replacing them, we discovered that the laws operated. The percentages took over—we lost attendance!

I began to look elsewhere to see if these three laws could be justified, and I discovered that there are a number of places where this justification can be found. In studying books on Sunday School growth, I saw this law in operation. In studying Eugene Skelton's book, *10 Fastest-Growing Southern Baptist Sunday Schools,* I saw instances of these three laws in operation over and over again. The book, for instance, tells of the Curtis Baptist Church in Augusta, Georgia. In 1970 this church had an enrollment of 2,513 wih an average attendance of 1,023. When the enrollment went to 3,575 in 1973, the attendance rose to 1,445. In other words, as that church gained 1,062 in Sunday School enrollment, it gained 422 in attendance.

The Calvary Baptist Church of Clearwater, Florida, in 1970 had an enrollment of 1,088. By 1973 it had enrollment of 1,608, a net gain of 520. The attendance during those three years rose from 530 to 874, a gain of 344 people.

The First Baptist Church of Paris, Texas, had an enrollment in 1970 of 1,641. In 1973 it rose to 2,142, a net gain of 501. The attendance likewise rose from 795 in 1970 to 1,015 in 1973, or a gain of 220. I could list many others that Dr. Skelton mentioned in his book, each proving this very same thing.

I was in Lake Charles, Louisiana, where Ray Raddin is pastor of the Boulevard Baptist Church. He gave me these statistics. He said that before ACTION in December of 1974, "We had an enrollment of 619 with an average attendance of 269. After we had ACTION a year later, our enrollment was 778, a gain of 159. Our attendance was 358, a net gain of 89."

Richard Kay is director of The Church Services Division of the California Baptist Convention. In a letter to Grady Cothen of The Baptist Sunday School Board, Mr. Kay said: "October was the preparation time for our churchwide enrollment week. The week was November 2-9. We also completed three weeks of intensive follow-up. During the November 2-9 enrollment week, we had sixty-six people in the Task Force, thirteen who enlisted by telephone and thirteen young people actively involved in the emphasis. The pastor worked all week enrolling members for his class. We enrolled 248. On the following Sunday, eighty-four of the new enrollees were in attendance. Our attendance increased week by week."

Each story verifies these laws of attendance. To return to my own and the Riverside story, I formulated the concepts and made some predictions. The interesting thing is I thought I had found something new. But that was not the case. Enrollment, however, had not received the emphasis it should. In fact, I am convinced that we can never build a Sunday School or a church, except in extreme cases, without an aggressive enrollment emphasis. It's like growing a tree without a root system. We must have the root system. We must have enrollment.

Therefore, I pulled enrollment out of its hiding place and placed it at the forefront of our program. My belief became reality in the months ahead. When we began this enrollment emphasis, Riverside Baptist Church, Fort Myers, where I had pastored for sixteen years, had an enrollment of approximately 1,000 with an average attendance of about 430. Within the first ten months while we were experimenting, not realizing what was taking place, we had a net increase of Sunday School enrollment to 1,650. The average attendance climbed to 650. In the eleventh month I put together all of the ideas that we had discovered would work, discarded the others, and we decided to see what would happen in a four-week period of time. We enrolled a net of 720 new Sunday School members, raising the enrollment to 2,300. Our attendance rose to 900. This was without a special promotional emphasis, simply through enrolling people in Bible study and letting them know we loved them and wanted them to attend.

At this time we had to cease enrolling new people. We ran out of space and teachers! We gave our attention to strengthening our ongoing Bible study program, enlisted additional workers, and trained them! We reorganized and enlarged our Sunday School along the basic Southern Baptist Convention plan; we studied and adjusted our space. Then we launched another enrollment campaign.

Our Sunday School director encouraged me to make this one small—we did not have additional room for many new people. So we had a one-Sunday afternoon emphasis and enrolled 407 new Sunday School members. This carried our enrollment to 2,700, our average attendance to 1,150.

I discovered through my own experience that what I had believed was true. I looked at these laws of attendance and realized that we could have about 50 percent of our enrollment present, no matter how many we enrolled. And the sobering thought came to my mind: the people are waiting for us to come to them.

We had to have about 50 percent absentees in order to have 50 percent present. When we had 1,000 people enrolled, we had somewhere in the neighborhood of 500 people present, 500 people absent. We had between four and five hundred people present. When we reached an enrollment of 2,700, we had approximately 1,200 people present and about 1,500 people absent. But I did not put on a campaign to erase the names of the 1,500 people who didn't come. For I realized that the attendance law was real.

I discovered something else—that all of a sudden my church, the church which I had struggled to grow for many years, grew like I felt Jesus wanted it to grow. I had wanted a large attendance in Sunday School, and with all the promotional gimmicks I had never achieved this for more than one Sunday at a time. Then all at once we had more than we could take care of. It came about because we enrolled persons.

With the same preaching, the same auditorium, the same promotion, the same music, the same everything, we had more people than we could seat in the worship services. When people came for Sunday School and Bible study, they stayed for the worship service. We had to go to two worship services to accommodate the people. All of the organizations of our church grew because we now had a larger reservoir from which to draw.

Money came, too. As I said to my people, "You cannot get more blood than the turnips have." We were already getting all of that blood. What we needed was more turnips! Our offerings more than doubled without any kind of special stewardship campaign. Baptisms–we won to Christ more than three times as many as we did before we started the enrollment emphasis, and this was without a revival meeting. When we enrolled the people in Bible study, when they attended, when they studied and prayed, God's Holy Spirit took charge, the people were convicted and saved.

In a later chapter I'll talk more about the evangelism part of enrollment. For now let me reemphasize my conviction–the best way to grow the church that Jesus needs is to start with the root system: enrolling people in Bible study. Other churches have found the same thing to be true. In this book it would be impossible for me to relate the stories of hundreds of churches which have used the same basic concept and seen an unbelievable growth take place. But let me mention a couple of them at this point.

A mission church in Tucson, Arizona, had eighty-five people enrolled in the Sunday School, but during the week of ACTION they enrolled 135 more and doubled the Sunday School attendance the very next Sunday. In addition to this, their worship service doubled, and so did their offerings.

Paul D. Carmichael, Jr., pastor of the Lee Street Baptist Church, Valdosta, Georgia, wrote: "Crowds, power, victory. These are the words which are surely appropriate for these days in the life of our church.

"I write to let you know a few of the immediate results of our new Sunday School enrollment program which is called ACTION. First, we began our new Sunday School year with an enrollment of 657 in our Sunday School, and now five weeks later we have 868 enrolled. This is an increase of 31 percent.

"Secondly, our Sunday School workers are visiting diligently to encourage all the new enrollees to become active attenders. Thirdly, on the first Sunday after our ACTION emphasis we had 413 in attendance, and last Sunday, which was Miracle Day, we had 491 people for Bible study."

When he was pastor of the Tower Grove Baptist Church, St. Louis, Missouri, Mack Douglas discovered that you will baptize 75 percent of your net enrollment gain year in and year out. "Therefore," he said, "you must establish the plan of enrolling twice as many people in Sunday School in the next twelve months as you have for your baptism goal."

I do not know if that will be true following the ACTION plan, but in Riverside Baptist Church we won to Christ approximately 500 during the time when our enrollment increased a net of 1,700 from 1,000 to 2,700. This was approximately 33 percent a year. Though the Sunday School enrollment is not continuing to grow as rapidly now due to "retooling" of the organization, the number of converts in Riverside under the leadership of the new pastor, Bill Love, is averaging about five per week—250 annually. It pays evangelistically to enroll people in Sunday School.

I believe if it is the desire of the church to baptize 100 new people into their fellowship, they must enroll between two and three hundred new people in Bible study.

4.
Be Willing to Risk

Risk may not be the best possible word to express my feelings at this point. It suggests the military commander who must be willing to commit his troops, to send them into battle. General Thomas Jonathan Jackson, commonly called "Stonewall" Jackson, has always been a favorite character to me. He furnishes a good example of a commander who risked much by committing his troops. They earned the name that came to them, the foot cavalry, from the rapid marches to which he subjected them.

His campaign in the Shenandoah was remarkable. Using the Massanutton Mountain as a screen, he moved his troops from one place to another in rapid succession, first losing himself to his Federal counterpart, Nathaniel Banks, and then falling upon Banks' troops unexpectedly. By keeping his intentions to himself, limiting his communications mostly to things past, being willing to risk his troops when he saw an opportunity to overcome or even confuse his enemy . . . "that enthusiastic lunatic," as one of his brigade commanders, General R. S. Ewell, admiringly called him, protected Lee's flank and prevented a Federal advance upon Richmond. But it could not have been done without *risk*.

In quite another realm, a businessman must venture

to create opportunity and success. Money invested in plants and goods involves risk, but without the venture nothing can be gained.

In 1928, Henry Ford led his company to drop the famous Model "T" in favor of the more advanced Model "A." The new model was an instant success. Several years later Ford came out with the Model "B," but failed to capture the imagination of the public. It might not have been called a failure, but the Model "B" lasted only a short time, one year. However, it led to the Ford V8, for many years a spectacular success. In fact, Ford still uses basically the same motor. Ford again ventured with the Edsel, only to fail. However, this car opened the way to the Thunderbird, Mustang, and Pinto, all successful in capturing large portions of the market.

A better word for risk in a church program is *faith.* Seeking God's guidance and the Spirit's leadership in devising a strategy, we then move ahead—believing God will give the increase. The risk factor is there, as it must be anytime a program in proposed. The fainthearted cannot try; the risk factor is too great for them.

But as Stonewall Jackson said to one of his generals, "Don't take counsel of your fears," a pastor must be guided not by his fears, but by the challenge of the task and the promise of God to give strength.

What are some of the risks involved in a major enrollment venture by a church?

People may accuse the church of playing the "numbers game." This accusation too often is leveled at all Southern Baptists and at growing churches too often by other Southern Baptist brothers. However, the reaching of large numbers of people seems to be the answer, the best answer, to such an accusation. What is wrong with the numbers game? Jesus fed all the 5,000 men present when he kept on breaking the loaves. He even numbered the group. If one does not play the numbers game, where does he go with his ministry?

A second risk—or at least a second possible accusation—is the neglect of quality in the program. One needs to ask: just what is a quality church program? Is it a sophisticated one? Is it one that has the finest equipment ready to be used? Is it one that uses the best—or at least the most recent—principles in its religious education program? Is it one where the Sunday morning groupings reveal a homogeneous, well-mannered, scrubbed-bright-and-clean group of boys and girls? Or is a quality program one in which the people are attuned to the command of Jesus to take the gospel to all people? Where concern for people is evidenced along with concern for methods of teaching? Can there be quality of a program where there is no emphasis on quantity, no emphasis on reaching every possible person for Christ?

A third risk is the possible lowering of the average attendance. The average over the entire Southern Baptist Convention is 52 percent. Some churches may be smaller; some may be larger. I've dealt with this at length in an earlier chapter. However, whatever the average attendance level in any given church, the risk is real that the enrollment of large numbers of people may cause the average to decline. If the church is more interested in averages than anything else, this risk may be extremely great. Some will reject an enrollment program because of the possibility of seeing this average decline. They prefer the seeming quality of a high attendance level to the actual presence of men and women, boys and girls.

Yet, look at the alternatives. With no enrollment emphasis at all, the enrollment gradually declines, and declining enrollment inevitably means a lower actual attendance. Does the church want a lower actual attendance? Some are satisfied to have that. With an emphasis on percentages, the tendency becomes to keep paring the rolls of excess or non-attending members. Here again the smaller roll seems to produce a higher percentage of attendance. What it produces in reality is a lower actual attendance.

If a church fastens its eyes upon the people yet unreached and asks itself a question, "How are we going to follow Jesus' command to reach as many as possible of these people?" it will be willing to risk a lower percentage figure for the higher actual attendance.

Another risk is that many of the new people may not be "our kind of people." Many churches are located in changing neighborhoods. Many are yet located in the inner cities. Many are being surrounded with apartments. These churches face the challenge: what to do about the different kinds of people who live around us?

First Baptist of Hialeah, Florida, is an example of this kind of church. This church found itself in the midst of a large and growing Latin population, its community filling with refugees from Cuba. The church asked itself what was its responsibility. To send money to foreign mission endeavors? Yes. But more! To reach the mission field all around its doors. The church selected to do both. It continued mission gifts; it also organized a department for those who speak the Spanish language. At the same time, the church welcomed into its fellowship all Latins who wanted to be in an English-speaking service.

The Spanish department of the church engaged in ACTION. In one Sunday afternoon the Spanish pastor, Ramon Diaz, led the church to enroll forty-eight new people in the Sunday School. By the end of the enrollment week this number had grown to sixty-six new people.

Tower Grove Church in St. Louis, Missouri, calls itself a mid-city church. During the past ten to fifteen years the community about this church has changed from upper middle class. The church wants to stay where it is located, however, and it wants to minister to the people who now live about it, as well as to its older members. In a recent ACTION campaign, the church visited several thousand homes in the immediate area. Two hundred people were enrolled; the attendance in Sunday School increased a dramatic 100 following this enrollment week. This church plans to engage in ACTION two or three times each year.

Another risk is overcrowding the buildings. The Immanuel Baptist Church in Cleveland, Mississippi, had 180 in attendance on the first Sunday of its ACTION week. The following Sunday attendance jumped to 380. This church called the state Sunday School office. "Please come and help us," they asked. "We have a problem." Bryant Cummins, state Sunday School Secretary, came with his staff. After looking at the space and the new enrollment figures, their recommendation was to go from one to two Sunday Schools on Sunday morning.

What a day! When churches must maintain two Sunday Schools to reach the people whom they can enroll in Bible study. Yet, some churches might prefer not to run the risk of having to make this provision.

Still another risk is the possibility of footdragging and

criticism by the more staid members of a congregation. "We have never done it that way," has been called "the seven last words of the church!" by Ralph Neighbour, Jr. But still they're too often heard. A pastor, Sunday School director, and progressive leadership must decide whether those who have too little faith to see what God can do will determine the direction of the church program, or whether the church will be led and directed by the Holy Spirit.

Perhaps there are other risks. At Riverside we decided the risk was well worth taking. We faced these same risks. Every one of them. But our decision was that reaching more people for Jesus was worth doing even if we lost a few percentage points, crowded classrooms a little, were inconvenienced with two Sunday Schools, and lost a few people who wanted more culture and class.

Can you afford not to take a risk? This really means, do you have faith enough to trust the God who commands you to go? And do you have faith God will lead you through?

5.
Have Courage to Change

Automobile manufacturers bring out new models year by year just for the sake of change; planned obsolescence, they believe, promotes sales. The changes often are no more than mere "face lifting." Real improvement is questionable or doubtful. Yet, never to change would be tragic. Then there could be no improvement. So with a church. Healthy and vigorous changes develop out of older established truths, methods, and programs, retaining the good of the old while seeking more effective means of getting kingdom work accomplished.

ACTION did not spring full grown; it developed from a basic idea and a basic desire to reach more people. Nor has it reached perfection—it still is developing. The plan will remain the same: direct and simple enrollment procedures. Tools, handles, and adaptations may be added from time to time.

At one time, Bible study for the people of a church was a novel idea. Preaching then was the main approach a church used. When Bible study was suggested as a companion activity for a church, it was so new and so unusual, some churches rejected it altogether. At the same time Bible study through the Sunday School was introduced, another new idea made its appearance: churches cooperating or working together for the promotion of mission enterprises. Some churches rejected this concept, also. In fact, the churches which refused to accept one of these ideas usually rejected the other, too. As their opposition to these novel ideas developed, they sought—and to their satisfaction found—a doctrinal basis for their stance. They justified their position by taking refuge in hyper-Calvinism, so strict as to become almost fatalism, if not wholly.

They began calling themselves "Primitive Baptists," even though a study of "primitive" Christian practices in the New Tesatment shows incontrovertibly that these early Christians and early churches gave themselves to Bible study *and* were also devoted to extensive mission enterprises. New Testament study also reveals that these missions were as often cooperative endeavors as they were the works of single churches.

The churches that emphasized Bible study and missions began growing. They became the mainstream of Baptist life, which developed into the people now known as Southern Baptists. Is it too much to say their willingness to change, as the Holy Spirit led, was one of the characteristics that brought them to their present greatness?

The development of the all-age Sunday School was another novel idea at one time. Some churches believed Bible study was good not only for children but for all people. They developed departments and classes for youth and adults.

Likewise, the grading of adults at one time was a new and novel idea. Many of those who read this book can remember some of the struggles taking place in churches as they debated whether to organize age-graded classes for adults in their Sunday Schools. Yet, those churches unafraid to make this change did age-grade adults and soon found themselves reaching more of this age group than ever before. Close grading made smaller classes possible, and smaller classes made concern possible for all people, as well as for each person as an individual. Churches able to adjust became greater churches in part because of their willingness to change.

Change should not be for the sake of change only. Nor should it be wild and uncontrolled, subject to whims and desires of any and every church member. It should be thoughtful and serious, guided and controlled by foundational convictions and led by the Spirit's presence in the church.

ACTION is such a change. It changes the place Sunday School enrollment has as an emphasis in the thinking of the church. It changes the enrollment procedures of a church. It creates a new attitude toward percentages as far as attendance is concerned. It changes the manner in which the church seeks to enroll people in its Bible study. It turns the eyes and actions of the church toward the community outside, rather than to the group to which it now ministers.

When a person first hears of ACTION, he usually asks that the whole concept be repeated; he thinks he must have missed something when it was explained. He listens, and a puzzled expression comes to his face. ACTION is different. It involves change.

ACTION is true to the primary purpose of the Bible teaching program of a church: to reach more people for Bible study, for Christ, and for church membership. It does not undermine any of the established and proven laws and principles of Sunday School growth and development.

Actually, it undergirds them. It substitutes nothing for excellent Bible teaching; rather it heightens the need, the absolute necessity for good teaching. But it does suggest change.

This change is a newer and bolder emphasis upon enrollment. A church comes to see and acknowledge the importance of enrolling large numbers of people as it sees and understands the necessary relationship between enrollment and all else a church does. Then a church can work for enrollment with real enthusiasm and joy.

Change is a healthy thing for an individual, as well as for a church. Bedrock convictions are needed, as needed as a backbone for a person. The life of a church, as well as the life of an individual, needs some unchanging principles on which to build. But changes and adjustments can be made without sacrificing any of these. The strong person discovers ways to reach his goals, not in conflict with his basic convictions and commitments, but in ways to strengthen and support them.

6.
Don't Be Afraid to Fail

I've always loved the game of baseball and have admired—almost inordinately—many of the baseball greats. One of the greatest of all was the "Bambino," Babe Ruth. Somewhere long ago I heard the following story about him.

On a beautiful Saturday afternoon in the year 1927, 35,000 fans gathered in Shibe Park, Philadelphia. Suddenly the packed stands began giving Babe Ruth the "razzberry." "Lefty" Grove, one of the greatest left-handed pitchers of all time, had just struck the Babe out on three pitches. It was the second time he'd done that in the afternoon. Two runners were on base.

As the powerful slugger returned to the bench, accompanied by the howls and jeers of the crowd, he stopped and looked up into the stands with a small smile on his face. Unruffled by the noise, he doffed his cap politely, wiped his sweaty forehead, and stepped down into the dugout.

The eighth inning found the "Bambino" at bat again. The situation was critical, with the Athletics leading the Yankees, 3 to 1. The bases were full, and two men were out. As the Babe selected his favorite bat and took a swing or two with it en route to the plate, the crowd rose in excitement.

"Strike 'em out again," the fans chanted to Grove. As the big southpaw strutted around the box, it was easy to see he thought he would.

Mickey Cochrane, the A's stellar catcher, crouched behind the plate and gave the sign. The crowd held its collective breath as the pitcher wound and rewound. Suddenly he turned the ball loose. Across the plate it moved with lightning speed. The Babe struck. It was a foul tip.

"Stee-rike One," the umpire roared.

The crowd became hysterical, then quiet, as the catcher signaled a second pitch. Grove wound the ball and pitched. The ball was too fast to follow.

Again Babe Ruth swung–and missed. He went to his knees in a cloud of dust; he'd literally swung himself off his feet. He sprawled on the ground for a moment and then slowly came to his feet, a grin on his face as he brushed the dirt from his trousers. He gave his hands a final rub on his seat and got himself ready for the next pitch.

Grove delivered the ball so fast none of the fans saw it. In only a split second, everyone knew what had happened. The Babe swung, and this time he connected. That ball would never come back. It disappeared over the scoreboard and cleared the houses across the street; it was one of the longest home runs in the history of baseball.

As Babe Ruth trotted around the diamond behind the other runners in what proved to be the game's winning run, he received a standing, wild ovation from everyone, including those who'd razzed him only a few minutes earlier. The expression on his face was exactly the same as the one he'd worn when he returned to the box the first two times.

Later in the season, someone asked him what he did when he dropped into a batting slump. "Just keep swinging," he replied. "Each time I strike out, I know I'm that much closer to the one I'll hit." In his lifetime he hit 714 home runs to become the "Sultan of Swat." But he also struck out 1,330 times. He owned the strike-out record even though little is ever said of that. But the truth to be seen is this: had he been afraid he'd fail, he never could have knocked the first home run.

Fear of failure can keep you and your church from making even an attempt to do the things which will bring success to your work and honor to Christ. Fear of failure will keep you in the same pattern or rut of the usual. Safe. Unimaginative. Humdrum. That can be failure by default.

There are other ways to fail—many of them. Grab a pencil and a sheet of paper, and jot down some of those ways. Such as being a drifter, being carried along by the current. In taking this route to failure, simply avoid like the plague any kind of goal, short-range or long-range. Just aim at nothing; you'll hit it every time.

Procrastination is a short and easy route to failure. Never do anything today you can put off until tomorrow. Wait until you have all the facts in. Since you'll never have all the facts, you'll never be compelled to act. This is the direction some take on ACTION. Having heard of the enrollment plan, they see what it has done and is doing for many churches. They see the advantages to be gained from using ACTION. But they feel the time is not ripe. They'll think about it for a while and study it more closely. Nothing happens.

Negativism is a sure formula for failure. Of course, ACTION has some weak points. Even though the Holy

Spirit works with and uses men, any plan has weaknesses. But spend the time searching for the weaknesses, and you'll have no time left to see the strength. Unfortunately, many of us were negative thinkers long before ACTION made the scene. Every suggested program has its cracks and flaws as far as the negative thinker is concerned.

Another shortcut to failure is to sell yourself short. Think constantly about your weaknesses and your past failures; be sure and tell others about them. You'll be afraid to venture from the on-deck circle to the plate with a bat. You may be sure that even after striking out two times, Babe Ruth walked up to the plate already seeing that ball sailing into oblivion just after he connected his bat with it. Failure need not be introduction to another failure; it may be a prelude to success.

But of all the well-traveled paths to failure, the one most often used is not trying. Often the fear of failure is camouflaged with other words such as *we've never done it that way,* but these really are an excuse for not trying. Someone wryly observed that only those who try, fail. Yes, and only those who try, succeed.

Really, all of life is a venture. Churches must not risk their main convictions, but they need not guard and protect with their lives their staid and static approaches. If they are to grow, they must be willing to try something new when opportunity arises. In Riverside we discovered that tradition dictated how people should be enrolled in our Sunday School. It was too difficult to join the Sunday School; in fact, it was more difficult to become a part of a Bible study department or class than it was to become a member of our church. All a person needed to do to join the church was to listen to the pastor preach, walk down the aisle, fill out a card, and be received into the fellowship. Not so with the Sunday School.

There we required a person to attend three times before being enrolled. Some churches never expected this. Some which once followed this practice have broken away from it; these will enroll new people the first time they attend. But not us. Tradition dictated to us, and we obeyed its strictures even when it meant doing something we felt was not quite right.

Then we came up with our new enrollment concept. Even then, before we ever started, some were afraid. "Andy, do you think it will work?" they asked.

My answer was frank. "No," I said. "But it's better than the plan we have now." You see, we had no enrollment plan whatsoever until then.

Little did we know how well the new plan would work. As we enrolled people by the dozens, and then by the hundreds, we realized it would indeed work. However, my point here is that we had to risk something in order to prove the plan was God's plan and would do for our Sunday School what we'd so desperately longed to see.

Sometime ago I was in one of the many ACTION interpretation meetings I've conducted. The specific place is immaterial. The minister of education of one of the stronger churches approached me, saying he had something to share. I smiled–I was happy to listen.

"When I first heard of the concept I didn't believe it would work," this young minster of education began. "Our church doesn't take many risks. We're old and staid." He smiled wryly and looked to see whether I wanted to hear the rest of the story.

Of course, I did. I knew he had something good to

say, or he likely wouldn't have been present and certainly wouldn't have spoken to me.

"The more I saw of the plan, the more I liked it," he continued. "So I decided to put it into a test tube. Two staff members and I would quietly go to work. We would enroll exactly fifty people and see what happened. That way we'd run little risk. No one would know if we failed."

I nodded. I understood his fear of failure.

"Well, we enrolled these people through the week, fifty of them. The following Sunday morning thirty-one of those we enrolled were present in our departments and classes. We couldn't keep it a secret." He grinned sheepishly. "Andy, tell us how to do it; we're ready to do it right," he concluded.

A church will never fill the facilities it fails to provide; it will never reach people with a plan it fails to follow and use. But no church needs to fear failure as long as it uses plans and programs to reach people and touches their lives with love. Enrolling them in Bible study because of loving concern, we can fill all the room we are able to provide.

An evangelist was to conduct an ACTION revival in a church. Arriving the latter part of the week before the revival was to begin on Sunday, he discovered the church had made little or no preparation. The ACTION program was so radical they could see nothing but failure. They let their fear of failure stop their progress.

The evangelist, their leader for the week, wise in the ways of church leaders, refused to be upset at them. He shared with them what he knew was happening in many other places, including accounts of the things he'd seen happen in his own ministry. Soon those church leaders accepted the program; they decided to go ahead, even running the risk of failure because of late preparation.

All Friday afternoon they worked, preparing enrollment cards and the packets for visitation on Sunday. On Saturday morning, when their eight bus workers arrived at the church to go visiting, they launched the program. They enrolled people all day long, stopping at every house on each of the bus routes long enough to ask the parents of bus children to enroll in the Bible study program of the church.

"We're happy to have your children. Now we'd like to enroll you in our Bible study program," they said. The previous high attendance on the bus routes had been 345 riders; on the next morning more than 650 crowded onto the eight buses. In addition a large number of regular riders missed the bus; they rode to church with their parents, who were attending the very first time.

This church, as does every church going into ACTION, recognized there is a possibility of failure. If they were to fail, they wanted it to be not from inaction, but *in action.*

ACTION provides the action that does not fail. Less than one percent of the churches engaging in ACTION have failed to realize outstanding success.

Dream a Fantastic Dream

"The hand of the Lord was upon me, and in a vision he took me . . . and set me down on a high mountain" (Ezekiel 40:1-2, TLB).

The purpose of this page is to lead you to dream your own fantastic dream for your Sunday School. Think and pray as you complete the following form. Then formulate your own fantastic dream for your church.

List the number of church members______
List the number enrolled______
List the number not enrolled______
How many of these would you like to enroll this year?______
How many people in church field?______
How many enrolled in your Bible study?____
How many in all other Bible studies______
How many available for Bible study?______
How many would you like to reach?______
Your present Bible study enrollment______
How many would like to enroll?______
Dream a little—how many can you dream of enrolling?

7.
Remember the Basics

When a football team begins its spring practice, it is a long time until the first game in the fall, but the team is laying the foundation for games it hopes to win then. The coaching staff leads the players in the basics of the game: running, blocking, and passing. Over and over each player practices these basics or fundamentals. If he can do these things well, he will be able to perform in the intricate plays yet to be developed.

A Sunday School also has certain basics or fundamentals. Every special plan or program relies in large part upon these basics for its success. Every emphasis likewise depends upon them.

The basics of Sunday School work have never been stated better than in the form given by Arthur Flake. Known as "The Flake Formula for Sunday School Growth," this formula seems to have been used either instinctively or deliberately by every Sunday School that has achieved growth. No Sunday School that has used this pattern or design for growth consistently has failed to grow.

The plan has five simple ideas: *locate the prospects, enlarge the organization, enlist and train the workers, provide the space, and go after the people.*

Using this plan or approach, Arthur Flake, then a young businessman, increased both enrollment and attendance in his Sunday School–First Baptist Church of Winona, Mississippi–approximately 500 percent in a short period of six months. This attracted wide attention, and soon Flake was in demand as a speaker and leader. Later he became the Sunday School director (called superintendent at the time) of the Sunday School at First Baptist Church of Fort Worth, Texas. This school also experienced phenomenal growth. Soon he became a field worker in Sunday School methods for the Sunday School Department of The Baptist Sunday School Board, a position he retained for the remainder of his life.

In this capacity, through the area served by the Southern Baptist Convention, he introduced these principles of growth to Sunday Schools. Wherever these were used, Sunday Schools grew, and strong churches developed. Southern Baptists experienced an era of remarkable growth in Sunday School enrollment. Many churches grew in fantastic leaps and bounds. Literally thousands of churches caught a vision of what God could do through them and with them to reach the waiting masses of people.

Later the "Laws of Sunday School Growth" were developed by J. N. Barnette and his staff. Barnette then was secretary of the Sunday School Department of The Sunday School Board. These laws were not designed to replace the formula for growth, but rather to undergird and interpret it. They grew out of extensive studies of growing Sunday Schools. They made possible a better understanding of the dynamics of growth as developed by the growth formula. There were seven of these laws:

1. The law relating to the enrollment stated that enrollment seldom reached a figure greater than ten for each church-elected worker in the Sunday School worker group.

2. The law relating to new classes stated that new classes grew faster, enrolled more new members, produced more baptisms, and provided more additional workers than the older, more established classes.

3. The law relating to size of classes stated that classes usually reach their maximum size, as far as attendance is concerned, within a relatively short period of time.

4. The law relating to grading stated that age was the best basis on which to grade and organize a Sunday School. Later it was recognized that this law might add that school grade is an acceptable means of grading children yet in school.

5. The law relating to promotion states that the way to maintain the grading system is with an annual promotion. Without this, the grading system soon disintegrates.

6. The law relating to buildings states that the building sets the pattern of the Sunday School organization. This does not mean, as has often been inferred, that a Sunday School inevitably will grow to the size of the building it uses; rather it means that the Sunday School cannot grow beyond the building it uses.

7. The seventh and final law of growth states that visitation is related to the growth pattern of the Sunday School. Where there is little or no visitation, growth is limited seriously.

Dr. Barnette and the Sunday School Department staff did not intend for the laws of growth to replace or render outmoded the Flake formula for growth. Nor is there any intent for the ACTION enrollment program to replace either the Flake formula or the laws of Sunday School growth. Based upon studies of how Sunday Schools grow, the formula and the laws will not change.

ACTION is not another gimmick. It is a program that is based upon the very heartbeat of Sunday School growth. It is a Bible-based program of outreach. It is a plan to achieve permanent growth, as we "go out into the highways and hedges [streets and lanes] and compel [love] them to come in."

When we go to the people of our communities, love them, express a desire to have them with us, they will come. There is a vast difference between knocking on a door and saying to someone, "Would you please give us some information about your family?" and going to that door and saying, "We want you and would love for you to join us."

The only denomination in the history of Christianity to enroll over 7,000,000 people and teach 3,500,000 of these each week in Sunday School is the Southern Baptist Convention. The methods and organizations used to accomplish this are fundamental. Some of these have been questioned by critics, but until someone reaches more people for Christ, for Bible study, and for salvation, I do not feel that there are any valid criticisms.

At the risk of repeating, I mention some principles I have found true in my experience of actually growing a great Bible teaching ministry. These principles produce growth, stability, and effectiveness.

First, the pastor must be the pastor of the Sunday School. I am afraid that in some instances pastors have felt they had more important things to do. But in my experience of thirty years in the Baptist pastorate, I have yet to see a Sunday School reach the people and accomplish its goals unless the pastor was the pastor of the school.

Second, attendance grows in proportion to enrollment. Between 40 and 60 percent of the enrollment is the average attendance. One of the greatest needs is to increase the enrollment, so the attendance will have a chance to grow. In fact, this is the reason and purpose for the ACTION enrollment emphasis.

Third, we must have adequate trained leadership. We have found that approximately one worker for every ten Sunday School enrollees is needed. These care for the teaching, visiting, and discipling of the students. Without this kind of leadership, it is difficult to sustain quality. No school system would permit too large a number of students in ratio to the number of teachers. We feel the same rule applies in our work. And no school system would permit untrained people to instruct teachers. However, this is being experienced in some of our Sunday Schools. It seems to me that every worker should be required to complete some instruction before beginning to lead or teach students in Bible study.

Fourth, adequate space must be secured if the church is to be effective and is to continue to grow. Multiple use of space is recommended as far as possible, but even this is not the complete answer. No school is what it should be, if the workers do not have a personal relationship, interest, and contact with the students. This is accomplished only by personal visitation.

Of course, the indispensable element of all Sunday Schools is the teaching of the Word of God and the lifting up of Jesus Christ.

May I share with you a personal testimony? In the Riverside Baptist Church there was a small, but rewarding annual growth. However, nothing compared to what there should have been. I did almost everything I knew to promote Bible study, but the Sunday School still did not reach out and touch the lives of people as it should have.

Realizing that church growth is not only numerical, but spiritual, I placed great emphasis on exegetical preaching, Bible conferences, the mid-week prayer meetings, training of workers, and the like. In spite of all we did, it seemed we were beating the air. We were not really touching the lives of the people of our community who needed the touch of God. Visitation was mainly among our own Sunday School membership. The few who participated in evangelistic visitation reached some for Christ and his church, but we were not reaching the mainstream of humanity. Our church was stagnant. It surely was not a duplication of the New Testament church in growth.

It seemed that the more we turned our attention on ourselves in seeking a deeper life experience, the slower we reached out to the needy community. We discovered that the only way to *grow* deeper is to *go* deeper into the sin-infested community with a personal expression of love. We discovered that when a personal invitation to join our Bible study is coupled with love it produces, not only many students in Sunday School, but enriches those who work for Christ. This spiritual and numerical growth was the key which unlocked the door of church growth so emphatically that we could not contain the increase. Every good thing began to happen when we began to enroll people in Bible study. SUNDAY SCHOOL ATTENDANCE FOLLOWED.

As the enrollment grew from about 1,000 to 2,700, the attendance grew from about 400 to over 1,100. This was not accomplished by the use of attendance gimmicks. When people are enrolled and followed up with love, the attendance grows. What we had been unable to do with special high attendance days, we saw take place automatically when the laws of Sunday School growth took charge. WORSHIP SERVICE ATTENDANCE FOLLOWED.

As the Sunday School attendance increased, so did the attendance at the worship services. Without any special promotion, it happened. We had the same pastor, same order of service, same music program, and yet all of a sudden the house of worship was filled. We had to go to two morning worship services. When the people came for Bible study, they remained to worship the Holy One. ORGANIZATIONAL ATTENDANCE FOLLOWED.

The reservoir from which we drew attendance and participation grew considerably. As a result we saw the various church organizations grow. In our own church the music department increased from about twenty-five faithful members to about seventy-five. There was so much interest in music that the front of our sanctuary had to be remodeled to enlarge the choir loft. The musicians were enthusiastic about their participation. They injected a new, warm, fresh spirit in our services. One pastor told me that the Church Training program in their church increased in attendance about 100 per Sunday without any special effort. When I asked him why this growth occurred, he answered that they made a special effort to enlist the new people in the Sunday evening activities. The new Sunday School and morning worship service attendance responded. INCOME INCREASE FOLLOWED.

The tithes and offerings automatically followed growth. In our church the income more than doubled, and this was without a stewardship program. As I look back over this experience, if I had to do it again I would have promoted a tithing and offerings emphasis each year. It would have been beneficial to the new people and helpful to the older attendees.

Here is an interesting fact for you to consider in your own church. First, take your average Sunday School attendance, divide it into the church budget. Now take the figure that you got as a result of that division, and divide it by 52. This will tell you how much each average Sunday School attendee contributes financially to the Lord's work. Now if you enroll 500 people in Sunday School and approximately 50 percent of these attend, the attendance would be 250. Multiply 250 times the average offering given by your Sunday School attendees, and this will be approximately the weekly increase in giving when you have enrolled 500 people in your Bible study. That is one of the most interesting and blessed thoughts that comes from ACTION. I have seen this happen in churches all over America. North, south, east and west. What we found was this: if you need a place to put these people, they will pay for any building that you need. However, if you do not enroll them, you will not have a dime with which to do anything. EVANGELISM FOLLOWS.

More important than all the other remarkable growth is the fact that many people will make their decisions to follow Christ and unite with his church without a revival meeting. We saw about twice as many people saved in our church each year that we had ACTION. This does not mean that we do not believe in special evangelistic meetings—we do. But when God is blessing as he did, we just let God's work grow week by week.

In the sixteen years prior to this new enrollment emphasis, we had averaged about 100 baptisms a year. This was with one or two revival meetings each year. Without these and during this period of enrollment, we baptized almost twice that many a year. But this is no surprise. One of the big reasons we don't win more people to Christ is that we have not touched their lives with the Word of God. The Sunday School has always been the outreach arm of the church. We enroll an unsaved person, expose him to Bible study, pray with him, and watch the Holy Spirit bring conviction and conversion. When we enroll more lost people, then more lost people are saved. Three thousand people were saved on the day of Pentecost, because 3,000 lost people were present. We know that we win to Christ one person out of every 262 who are not enrolled in Sunday School. We know that we win to Christ *one out of three lost people who are enrolled in Sunday School.* This tells me we must enroll more people in Bible study. For the Scripture says, "Being born again . . . by the Word of God." Let's let the Word of God touch the lives of more people.

Nat Burns, minister of education for the First Baptist Church, Palmetto, Florida, wrote: "This approach to Sunday School enrollment and enlargement has drastically changed the life and ministry of our life and church." Here are some of his "for instances."

1. We enrolled 341 people in one week.
2. Our attendance went from 255 to 350 in one week.
3. We have had decisions in every service.
4. Our homebound ministry has enlarged.
5. Our workers are excited and involved.
6. We anticipate making several new departments by the end of the year.

Another pastor wrote: "We had seventy-two additions to our church during the associational year. And most of them were enrolled in the ACTION program first." Still another pastor wrote: "Over the last three months (since ACTION) we have had seventy-four additions to our church. The church has set a goal of 100 baptisms for the year."

It is true that there is a part of the church growth which cannot be diagrammed on a graph. This is the spiritual side. Without this there would be no church—only a club. The Holy Spirit's presence is indispensable. We do not always see this growth, but thank God it is there. "He who has begun a good work in you . . ." Our usual gauge of growth is the numerical gauge. We see increase and decrease in the attendance. Our desire is to witness an increase in Sunday School, worship services, the organizations, the finances, and the baptisms.

Unless the pastor is "super," I see no way to enjoy a numerical increase except to begin at the beginning—enrollment. We cannot grow a tree without roots. Enrollment is the root system. I had spent twenty-six years trying to grow a numerically and dynamically great church. And though we had enjoyed some success, I was always bothered by the fact that the church was not reaching people like the New Testament church. I used all kinds of promotional gimmicks. I was success-oriented. My hope was that those who were in attendance were growing in grace and in the knowledge of Jesus. But for years I had very little to indicate this was taking place.

This all led to frustration. I expect it is a frustration felt by thousands of other church leaders. If a church is not growing, the pastor so often becomes restless. The deacons and other church leaders feel they cannot sit idly by while the church goes down, and I'm afraid some bad decisions are made. Once we discovered a key of growth—enrollment—we found that the entire church grew without gimmicks. It is better to grow a church on the LEADERSHIP of the pastor than on the PERSONALITY of the pastor.

8.
Keep Your Plan Simple

"Write the vision and make it plain upon the tables," God said to the Old Testament prophet Habakkuk. "That he may run that readeth it" (Hab. 2:2). Might this not have been a direction to make the words so simple that every person would understand without fail? In any case, God's *methods* as well as his *message* need to be communicated with ideas and in words quickly and easily understood.

Upon his first coming to The Sunday School Board, this principle was recognized by Allen Comish, director of the Church Services and Materials Division. In speaking to the professionals of the division, he said "Simplify." "This is the cry from our churches, and it is common sense as well," he continued.

"Get the idea on one page," says Stanley Williamson of the Stewardship Commission of the Southern Baptist Convention. "If you can't get it on one page, keep working until you can express the essential idea pointedly and succinctly. Simplify."

I'm an old-fashioned believer in the old-fashioned gospel that has warmed this world's cold heart for two thousand years. But God's plan, beautiful as it was, was also a simple one. We should not be afraid to be simple, for simple is not necessarily shallow. In Riverside Church we wanted something all our people could understand almost as quickly as it was explained. And the Lord gave us such an idea. It is expressed in four words: anyone, anywhere, anytime, and agree.

We knew we made it too hard to join our Sunday School. In fact, it was more difficult to join our Sunday School than to join our church. Should that be true? We thought not. Anyone should be able to become a part of our Bible study fellowship. Therefore, our plan.

Its first word: *anyone.* Up until then, we enrolled in our Sunday School only individuals who had been present three Sundays in succession. But after the plan we would enroll anyone, whether he'd attended three Sundays, two Sundays, one Sunday, or none at all. If the individual had never been present but desired to join, we would enroll him as a full-fledged member of our Sunday School. And why not? People enrolled under this new concept would attend; we discovered later that percentage-wise, they would attend just as well as those enrolled under our former screening plan.

Our second word was *anywhere.* Up until then the only place we ever enrolled a person was in the Sunday School department or class room. I never heard of anyone being enrolled in the hall, in the sanctuary, or on the grounds of the church. We enrolled them in our Sunday School rooms and only in our Sunday School rooms.

But in the plan we would change that. We would enroll the lady in the grocery store, the man at his business, the student in his classroom or laboratory. We would enroll a friend, acquaintance, or stranger in his home, at a sporting event, on a fishing trip, or any other place we could

I'm happy and not without reason. And thousands of people share my enthusiasm over ACTION. (BSSB photo by Jim Lowry)

Top: **I travel 20,000 miles or more a month. Here's a blessed break.** ***Bottom:*** **I prize my collection of old Bibles. (BSSB photos by Jim Lowry)**

Top: **Two men from Riverside Baptist Church who have helped spearhead ACTION—(left) Frank Land and Dr. James E. Wright (Photo courtesy of Frank Land)** ***Bottom:*** **What a thrill it was for me to be with Dr. R. G. Lee and the late Mrs. Lee. (Photo by George Schupka)**

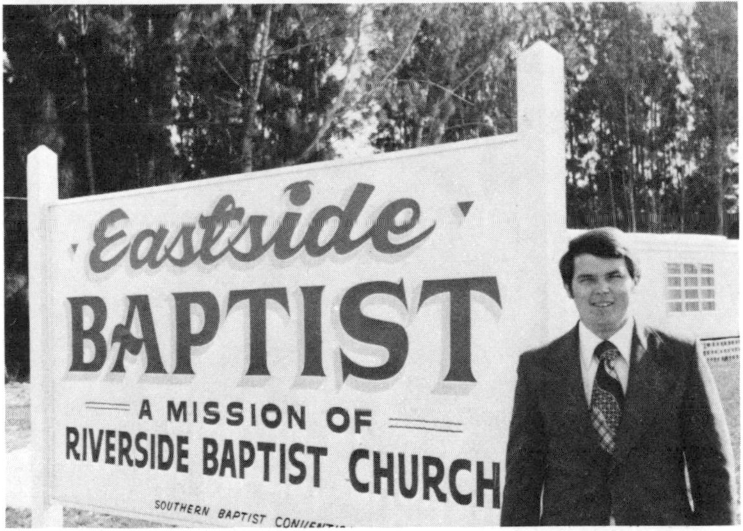

Top: The First Baptist Church of Eufaula, Ala., and L. Dale Huff, pastor—"ACTION showed that we are a church that cares enough to go to the people," says Huff. _Bottom:_ The mission of Riverside that resulted from ACTION—pastor Elmer Crews is shown. (Photo by Frank Land)

Top: **Guess what we're talking about. (BSSB photo by Jim Lowry)**
Bottom: **Larry Vowell, minister of education, points to results of ACTION at Mobberly Avenue church, Longview, Tex.**

Top left: Damon Vaughn, pastor of First Baptist, Bossier City, La., is sold on ACTION. (Photo by Cowen Studios, Shreveport) *Top right:* So is James A. Puckett, pastor of Harlandale church, San Antonio, Tex. *Bottom left:* My father-in-law, Boyd Haley, and his pastor, Dr. Tommy E. Lovorn, in front of First church, Cheraw, S.C. *Bottom right:* My home church, First Baptist of Cheraw

Top: **I'm dealing with the ABC's of ACTION. (BSSB photo by Jim Lowry)** ***Bottom:*** **Our going-away reception at Riverside, where we had served for nineteen years**

Top: **ACTION will pack your church's parking lot. (Photo by Frank Land)** ***Bottom:*** **Even though I have little time at home, we make it count. Our daughter, Sonja, is standing, and that is Eleanor on your right. Another daughter and a son are married. (BSSB photo by Jim Lowry)**

Ridglea Baptist Church (left), Stanley Kelley, pastor, and First Baptist Church of Atlanta, Ga., Charles Stanley, pastor, have conducted highly successful ACTION campaigns.

Top: **First Baptist Church of North Fort Myers, Fla., had a tremendous victory with ACTION. H. Fred Williams, pastor, is in the inset. (Photo by George Schupka)** ***Bottom:*** **Members of the Task Force enroll new members for Moberly Avenue church, Longview, Tex.**

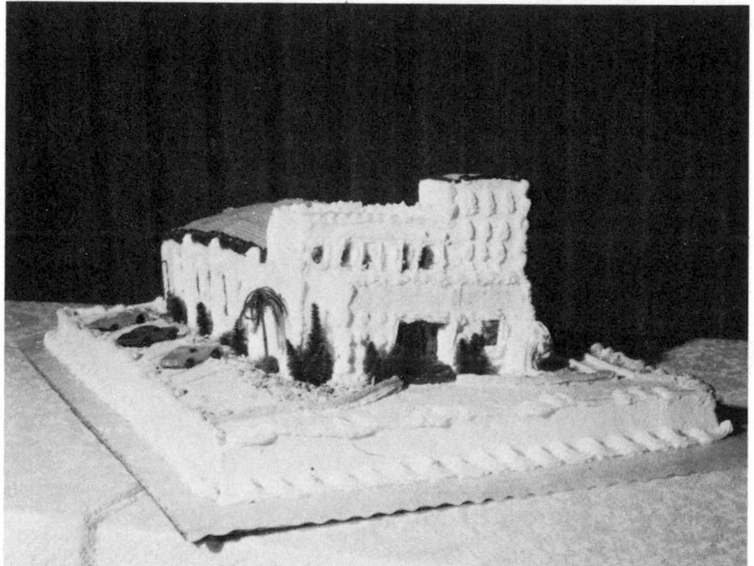

Top: **Riverside Baptist Church of Fort Myers, Fla.** ***Bottom:*** **Our going-away cake at Riverside—a sweet church indeed!**

find a person willing to be enrolled. Even though the person might not know the name of our church, we would enroll him. Then we'd tell him and tell him how to find us.

The third word was *anytime.* Our only time for enrolling a person had been between 9:45 and 10:45 on Sunday morning. I really had never heard of anyone being enrolled in Bible study before Sunday School started or after it ended. But now we would do it differently. No longer would we enroll people just during the "sacred hour." Now we would enroll them Sunday, Monday, Tuesday, Wednesday, Thursday, Friday, or Saturday.

Agree was our fourth word. The only requirement we placed upon joining our Sunday School was that the person must agree to become a member. We were interested in enrolling every possible person, but we would enroll only those who wanted to be members of our Sunday School.

The idea was as simple as the four words. And it was different from anything in my experience. "But why not?" I asked myself and my people. "Why not?" Our hands had been tied by an old traditional concept; now they would be loosed. By taking off the restrictions, we would give ourselves an opportunity to get the job done.

To be sure, we ran into problems. Some members of our church became upset because they didn't want "all those new people coming in." Some would come on the church buses, and some might even walk in. Many who had no church experience and knew nothing about what we believed might come. They wouldn't "know how to behave in church." Some teachers didn't want "all those names on the roll." Traditionally, they had "cleaned the rolls" once each year. They were afraid their grades or percentages might decline. We also faced that inevitable attitude: what we need is "not quantity but quality." Some insisted we "just talked about numbers." And so the objections ran. Some of our people had less than total enthusiasm for some of the aspects of our new approach; still, everyone understood the simple idea on which it was based.

As these problems arose, together we prayed about them to find God's answer. We did want new people because Jesus Christ died for all the people. And the people of our community whom we could reach, we *had* to reach. We did want all of those names on the roll, for we knew with 1,000 people enrolled and 400 in attendance, we had 600 people on the roll not attending on any given Sunday.

With 2,000 people enrolled, we believed we would have 800 people in attendance Sunday by Sunday. If we had 1,200 absent, that was part of the price we must pay for the larger attendance. We knew we could have between 40 and 50 percent of our enrollment present; we also knew that we had to have that 50 to 60 percent absent to have the other. Actually, we reached 2,700 enrollment, and we did see our attendance rise to nearly 1,200. In doing this we lost nothing in quality. We wanted quality in our Sunday School work. In fact, our Sunday School director was Dr. Bob Anderson, a graduate of the University of Florida and Emory University, and for a number of years chairman of the school board in our county. He said to me many times after we began this growth that we had a better quality of teaching in our Sunday School than we had before the plan. For the people were *motivated* by growth.

There were those who asked, "When will we get enough teachers, because we don't have enough even now?" The answer? God always supplies the need, and we uncovered in our own church all of the faithful workers we needed. In fact, we discovered that in our church membership we had over 100 leaders who had certificates in training, but who had, for one reason or another, ceased work in the Sunday School. Many of these came back and became the leaders of the growth we had. That's how God works.

The characteristic common to most growing churches is their positive commitment to reaching people for Bible study, for Christ, and for church membership. This commitment can be called the common denominator of growth. Without exception, these churches interpret the Great Commission as reaching people, especially the lost, for Bible study. They make this the first priority of the church. They shape and evaluate their programs on the basis of one criterion—a thoroughgoing determination to reach people.

These churches eliminate "busy work." All extraneous matters are removed. They are trimmed back to the main task at hand. That task is outreach. Nothing else be it ever so good is allowed to interfere with this commitment. This is the yardstick by which these growing churches measure every activity. To this they have made a commitment.

Lew Reynolds, in speaking to the state Sunday School directors in Nashville in December, 1975, said, "People, please understand me. We do have a five-star program, but our new work will start with Bible study, not with a GA program, or a Training Union program, or even with a music program. The Bible study program will be the heart of it. And if we gear all of our forces and build on this foundation, success has already been assured."

It is my personal conviction that if we are to build in each of our communities the church that Jesus wants and needs, we must give our people guidance and direction in simple, easy-to-understand terms. Enrolling people in Bible study is a simple idea; we must not complicate it with too sophisticated programming, but keep it in terms the most uninitiated can understand. When our people feel the leadership of God's Holy Spirit, and when they understand how to do the task, they will respond.

9.
Involve More People

"Pastor, is there some way I can become involved in what you're asking our church to do?"

I looked at the lovely woman who asked me the question and wondered how to answer her. Mrs. David Strickland, Sr., for many years had been one of the most faithful and active women of our church. She had been a loyal member and officer of our Woman's Missionary Union, working long hours to prepare fine programs and lead our church to year-after-year success in the mission offerings.

She had been dependable on committees of all kinds, seldom if ever missing a meeting and doing with enthusiasm every assigned task. But most of all she had been one of the best Sunday School teachers any pastor could want. Now all that was in the past. She was well along in years but had served until her heart slowed down. She carried a pacemaker to keep it functioning. She could do no physical work of any kind. She could attend services on many Sundays, but that was all.

How I wanted to say to her that she could go out from door to door with one of the Task Force teams. But I couldn't do that, and I knew it. But there was something she could do.

"Yes, you can be involved," I answered. "There's something for you to do."

Her eyes beamed, and her always-present smile grew larger than life. I forgot her pacemaker. She didn't need to ask what she could do–her eagerness asked for her.

"You can be a telephoner."

"Of course I can." Her quick mind already knew what a telephoner could do. "I know at least twenty people I could call this very afternoon."

Mrs. Strickland began that day and refused to find a stopping place. Even after the week of enrollment ended, she kept on working. She continues to do this. She had invested her whole life in reaching people for Jesus Christ, and she wanted to be involved. Giving her an opportunity met a need in her life. Yes, we needed some people to work with me in the telephone ministry. There are some people whom we never could reach by knocking on doors. They live in places too difficult to reach, and they live in places removed from the areas we planned to work. So Mrs. Strickland's need coincided or corresponded to the need of her pastor and her church.

Beyond this she illustrated a truth about all work churches try to accomplish: the more people the leadership involves, the more and better the work accomplished. Involving people in reaching people is a key to happiness for church members. ACTION recognizes and uses this principle. As a leader, you can involve large numbers of people when you use ACTION, involve them in exciting, joyful, satisfying, and productive ministry.

Quite apart from ACTION, the Sunday School involves a large number of people in ongoing functions. Usually we think only of the teachers and suppose that a relatively few are involved, but there are many beyond these.

Every adult class should use an outreach leader. This person is asked by his church to be the administrative leader of the class. He has the responsibility of making it function as a Bible-teaching unit. But he also makes it function as a people-reaching unit and as a team for evangelism. The outreach leader can magnify his task; it is a large task with an outstanding opportunity. In addition, the adult class should have from two to six group leaders. These are the contact persons between the class and its members. Each class member is assigned to one of these group leaders, who becomes in a sense the class minister for that person, and for each person assigned to his group. Multiply the number of classes in your adult division by five; at least this many people are involved if the classes are fully organized.

Youth departments also have outreach leaders, but the class teachers call upon the youth themselves to help and assist in the visitation. Still larger numbers are involved in every youth department.

In children's and preschool departments, larger numbers of workers are suggested in ratio to the number of boys and girls enrolled, as low as one worker for each four members in the youngest departments. One of the workers in each department is designated as director and one as outreach leader. Other workers serve not only as teachers but also in much the same way group leaders do in the adult classes.

Since involvement creates a better chance for success, one of the steps in preparation for an ACTION campaign is and should be bringing the organization up to the suggested strength. Fill every vacancy. Create the groups in the adult classes if the classes do not have them already. Select and elect persons to serve as outreach leaders in the classes. Lead these outreach leaders to select and get into service the required group leaders. Just doing this is often enough to create an initial wave of excitement that is excellent preparation for the even more exciting things about to take place.

ACTION opens possibilities of involving even larger numbers of people. Mrs. Strickland was not the only person in Riverside Church who was physically unable to walk from house to house; there were others like her, and they reached literally scores of people by enlisting through the telephone.

Jane Markley was one of those persons. This woman is one of the most beautiful women I have ever known. She radiates with the love of Christ. Emotionally and spiritually she has grown as she reached out and touched others. Already in her seventies, she had never sold anything, but when she joined the ACTION campaign as a Task Force worker, she discovered her ability to "sell" Bible study. She began enrolling people and has never stopped. She probably has enrolled more people in Sunday School than any lay person I know.

The enthusiasm of Jane Markley and Mrs. Strickland was matched by the joy of the youth of Riverside Church. Larry Ferguson, the minister of youth for the church, secured the names of the entire student body in some of the schools. He then enlisted the youth of the church to work to enroll those young people not already engaged in Bible study. The young people came to the church and completed an enrollment card for every person whose name they had. They grouped these cards by geographical areas, organized themselves into teams, and began working, a driver and a non-driver on each working team.

In talking with those they visited, they discovered first whether the young person already was enrolled in a Bible study program. If so, they thanked him and destroyed the card. But if he were not already enrolled, they attempted to enroll him right then. Within a few days, this group of young people enrolled approximately 400 high school students.

Our church also involved a large group of young people in an enlarged bus outreach program using ACTION. We already had a small bus program. We were reaching only a few people and those with relatively little work. We invited every young person in the church to come on Saturday and have a part in enlarging the work of our five routes; 100 young people responded. We assigned twenty to each of the bus routes.

But our largest group of people was those involved in the Task Force, the people who went out with their assignments on Sunday afternoon and kept visiting through the week until each assignment was completed. My goal was fifteen Task Force workers for each 100 people already enrolled. I worked until I enlisted this many people.

The task to which they were assigned was not one requiring extensive training; I was able to do all that needed to be done in a short period of time just before I sent them out. Neither was the work difficult; every person who was willing to try was soon able to do his job and do it well. At least, well enough. Yet, it was vital to the work our church was attempting, it was strengthening to the emotional and spiritual growth of the people, and it was productive. It rendered a real service to the persons we enrolled. Without these Task Force members, those new enrollees may never have known the joy of participating in Bible study!

Some of the Task Force members were scared to death before they went out. But after I took a few minutes and explained to them what they could do, they went through our community like locusts through a wheat field, not missing anyone they could enroll in Bible study. When they returned later in the afternoon, they were more excited over what they'd accomplished than perhaps they'd ever been before. They wouldn't stop talking; they wouldn't sit down; they wouldn't go home. They wanted to share their experiences with me and with each other. They continued through the week, and when the week was over many of them wanted to keep the same work going.

They were as excited as the woman in a Texas church, according to John Sisemore, the director of the Sunday School Division of the Baptist General Convention of Texas. "She was on the telephone committee," says Sisemore. "On one afternoon she enrolled eleven people just calling wrong numbers!"

One of the secrets of ACTION success is a secret that works in any area of your church life: For success, involve people in reaching people.

10.
Visit to "Make Sales"

Shubal Stearns was the indomitable pastor of the Sandy Creek Separate Baptist Church of western North Carolina from 1755 to 1771. This church, the "mother church" of the Southern Baptist people, kindled the fire of concern and commitment that continues to burn brightly until this very day. It was the first of the great "reaching people" churches. Stearns was a small man but spoke in a pleasing, musical voice. But his secret was a manner of speaking convincingly and for a verdict. He expected those to whom he spoke to decide for Christ at the conclusion of his messages. And they did.

In a few years the church grew from sixteen to 606 members, while at the same time extending "arms" to literally dozens of communities where small groups could be gathered and would become churches themselves. Like a brushfire the flame of evangelism swept the western frontier. The one compelling reason was the manner of speaking adopted by all the preachers, following the lead of their "reverend old father," Stearns himself. They spoke for a decision. To put this in a slightly different context: they visited with a purpose; that purpose was to lead men to decide for Christ.

One of America's greatest insurance salesmen—and

one of the nation's richest men—describes his secret in a similar way. W. Clement Stone tells how he began selling insurance policies while still a teen-aged boy. For his first day at work, he was given a five-point set of sales instructions: (1) Canvass completely the Dime Bank Building [in Detroit], (2) Start at the top floor and call on each and every office, (3) Avoid calling in the office of the building, (4) Use the introduction: "May I take a moment of your time?" and (5) Try to sell everyone you call on.

The first day he sold only two policies. The second day someone suggested he never should ask for a person's time—just take it. He began selling without an apology for the time given him. That day his sales increased. Later, he learned he could not sell everyone, so he began spending with each person only the time needed to make the sale or to determine the sale could not be made quickly. Then sales zoomed.

The account reads almost like instructions to a group of ACTION Task Force workers as they go out to enroll people for Bible study. The key phrase is *visit with a purpose and work to achieve that purpose with every visit.*

The Oakview Baptist Church of High Point, North Carolina, had 319 in attendance in Sunday School on the Sunday morning ACTION was to be launched. Thirty-one visiting teams went out from the church that afternoon. By the close of the afternoon, 107 new people had been enrolled in the church's Bible study program. At a sharing service, an ACTION rally, that evening the reasons for the success became apparent.

"I had never visited for my church before," began one of those who spoke. The speaker smiled, and everyone knew her experience that afternoon had been a happy one.

"I didn't know if I could. But I knew I was going for a specific purpose, and I knew I could say something about the Bible study program of our church, and I knew to ask to enroll the people. I wouldn't forget that."

Almost everyone smiled with the speaker; their experiences that afternoon had been much like hers. They too were uneasy when they left the church, and they too reminded themselves that they were visiting for one purpose: to enroll people in Bible study.

"After the first few houses it became easier," the attractive woman continued. "Then I came to the house where the people said they wanted to be part of a Bible study program. I enrolled three people there and before I finished the afternoon enrolled four others."

Following her testimony a young man arose. "Six of us went to the college," he began. "We formed ourselves into three teams. We knew what to say: that we'd come to enroll them in our Bible study program. We enrolled twenty-three college young people." The church had no college department, but the announcement was made that the department would be launched the following Sunday morning. The church had two buses it had used for trip buses, and now one of these buses would be used to bring in the college young people.

Another woman, an older woman, spoke for herself and for her team worker in the afternoon's work. "We enrolled fifteen people," she reported. "One reason we could do this was because we knew we were visiting for a definite purpose."

Too many of our church visits are made with no purpose other than "to be sociable," that is to be pleasant and create and leave behind a good feeling toward the church. We assume this will do some good–and sometimes it does. We've even developed a "theology" or rationale for this kind of visitation: we call it "cultivative visitation." While cultivative visitation no doubt has value, it also helps us excuse or rationalize our almost complete failure to work for actual decisions, either when we visit or in our contacts with people already involved in the Bible study program.

Almost every visit should be for a purpose, for a decision. To "make a sale." This is one of the things I learned while working with ACTION in my church. After seeing this I began carrying two kinds of cards with me at all times.

First, I carried with me Sunday School enrollment cards, and I remained conscious that every person I talked with throughout the day needed to study the Bible. Therefore, I asked each one whether he was enrolled in Bible study, and if not, to give me the privilege of enrolling him in the program promoted and conducted by Riverside. On more than one day I was able to enroll a large number of people simply because every time I made a contact I tried to "make a sale." I wanted decisions, and I got them.

The second kind of card I carried with me was the church membership card. One of the personal goals I had set for myself was to lead at least one person to Christ each day. When I succeeded I wanted to have a church membership card in my hand. I wanted to talk to the new Christian about coming into church membership, and I wanted to give him an opportunity to complete the church membership card while I talked to him about how to unite with the church. Of course, I found many people needing to transfer their church membership; since I had the membership cards with me, it was easier to encourage them to follow through with this important decision.

Visiting for positive results is a secret of successful visitation. It is one reason for the success of the Task Force. When two people are assigned to a street, they knock on every door, and they ask for decisions; after making their brief presentation they ask the family to enroll in Bible study. They visit to "make sales."

I'm not sure I knew the truth of this chapter before the Lord gave ACTION to me and the people at Riverside Church. I may have discovered a great truth about visitation through what we did with ACTION those first times. Be that as it may, when our people began visiting for ACTION, they began visiting with a definite and specific purpose in mind.

Almost all visitation should be done in the same manner—with specific objectives in mind. Following enrollment the specific decision sought may be attendance the following Sunday, since every person enrolled is a prospect for attendance each Sunday. The desired decision may be to accept Christ as Savior or a decision to come into the fellowship of the church. Simply to see some other ways specific visitation may be done, let's follow a person from the time he is enrolled through some of the visits and contacts he may receive from the church.

First, the Sunday School teacher to whose department or class he is assigned will visit him. The teacher will welcome him to the class and place in his hands the literature, quarterly or curriculum piece, the class members use. The visit is specific—both the welcome and quarterly make it so. The visit is easy for the teacher to make because he knows exactly why he is calling. He also visits to secure the attendance of the newly-enrolled department or class member for the following Sunday morning. In most cases, this visit will be made toward the end of the ACTION enrollment week just before Welcome Sunday.

When new department or class members are enrolled at other times than during an ACTION enrollment week, as they will be when the church follows ACTION as an ongoing pattern for reaching new people, the department worker or class teacher still makes this call at the earliest possible time. It should always be before the first Sunday a person is in attendance, if this is at all possible.

About the middle of the following week this newly enrolled member receives a visit from his pastor. This will be in the form of a letter, not as good as a visit, but at least good enough to demonstrate the pastor knows about him and is concerned for him. Within a few weeks he will receive a face-to-face visit from the pastor. In this instance there may no "sale" to make; the pastor comes primarily to become acquainted and to communicate to the newly enrolled person a sense of belonging. Although the pastor works for no decision, the visit is still of tremendous value.

During the same week, the week after his first Sunday in his new class, the new enrollee receives a visit or a contact of some kind from the group leader to whom he has been assigned. If he is now in an adult class, his class has several groups, and each of these groups has a leader whose regular responsibility is contacting group members. If he is in a youth department, he may be contacted by his teacher. If he is a member of a children's or a preschool department, one of the department workers who teaches on Sunday mornings also serves as a group leader. Whatever department or class he has been assigned to has someone who will contact him. This contact may be a visit, or it may be a telephone call or letter the first week. Each week his group leader will contact him. If he has not received a personal visit the first week, he certainly will the second or third week. He soon will learn to expect that contact from his group leader each week.

Some time later, as a new quarter approaches, this member, now fully at home with his class and with a secure feeling of really belonging, may receive a visit from his teacher delivering to him the quarterly or piece of literature he will use in the new quarter. By this time the new member himself may be taking part in the literature delivery as one of the faithful members of the class. Likely he will be one of a record-breaking attendance at his Sunday School class and department the following Sunday morning.

One day his teacher may call for an appointment to talk to him about "something of greatest importance." This new member, now no longer really new, will guess what this is. His teacher calls to talk to him about being saved, about giving his life to Christ as Lord and Savior. This time his visitor does lead him to make a decision, the one which logically follows his first decision, to be enrolled as a part of the church's Bible study program.

Almost every visit has a purpose. All lead to the time of decision for Christ and church membership. The entire matter can best be summed up with a story which came to me from Frank Land. Frank is a member and deacon of the Riverside Church and gives himself freely in leading churches in weeks of ACTION. Let him tell this story in his own words.

"We had a school teacher over in South Carolina that was told by one of her pupils that she couldn't come to Sunday School some months prior to ACTION, but that she wanted to. It seems that as the assignment sheets were passed out, this school teacher was put down the street of this particular student, and as she walked up to the door she said, 'Oh, Lord, I'll be run off.' But as she rang the bell, and a man came to the door, she simply said, 'Hi, I'm your daughter's school teacher, but that's not what I'm here for.' And to make a long story short, she walked off enrolling the entire family, and now that child has a chance to come to Bible study. This young lady stood up during testimony time and simply said, 'Mr. Land, I was against this program. It doesn't make sense. I couldn't see how anybody was going to let us enroll them, never mind enrolling them in Sunday School, because they have not even been to church yet.' But she said, 'I went and I can hardly wait to go again tomorrow.' "

11. Demonstrate Enthusiasm

What makes the difference between success and failure? Often enthusiasm does. What can transform a "ho-hum" church into one bubbling over with excitement and challenge? Enthusiasm can. What is the magic ingredient without which even ACTION cannot work? Enthusiasm is.

What can bring happiness to the one who expresses it and joy to the one who sees it? Enthusiasm can. For the Christian, enthusiasm means to experience the joy of salvation and then to let that joy, as a gushing spring, run out and run over. The Greek words from which enthusiasm comes suggest its meaning. Those words? The word for in *(en)* and the word for God *(theos)*. Enthusiasm? It is the presence of God in us, springing up and overflowing to share spontaneously the joy of being saved and serving Christ. Others may take away some of this meaning, but for the Christian it's all this. Even more.

How does one come by this enthusiasm in his church program? Is being in ACTION enough? Perhaps. But it would be better to say that while a church should do all its work with enthusiasm, it should especially show abundant enthusiasm in doing ACTION. How can such enthusiasm be generated?

1. Believe in what you're doing. A sincere and abiding belief in the value and worth of any action or program underlies genuine enthusiasm for it and a carrying of it through.

A young man accepted a part-time job selling life insurance. Not long afterward he sold a large policy to one of his closest and dearest friends. The friend laughed at the time and said it was more than he could see a real need for, but he paid the first year's premiums.

In only a few weeks, he was killed in a tragic automobile accident. The young salesman, who was also music director of his church, went with the pastor to his friend's home to break the sad news to his wife. Later he sang for the funeral. A few days afterward he called at the home with a check large enough to cover necessary expenses and to explain the options his company offered as payment of the large policy. The young mother of three children wept. Then she explained the reason for her tears. "Jim," she said, "You're the best friend my husband and I ever had. Had it not been for your talking him into buying this policy, we'd have no way to care for ourselves now. Thank you for what you've done for us."

That young man later said he knew at that moment how he wanted to spend the rest of his life. He became a successful salesman and then a successful manager of a team of salesmen. The reason for his success? Enthusiasm for what he was doing. The reason for his enthusiasm? He believed in what he was doing with all his heart.

Should I make an application of this to our church programs? If they are meaningful and if they help people, why shouldn't we believe in them with all our hearts? I know this is especially true of ACTION. It is a program that does something for churches and does something for every single person we are able to enroll in Bible study.

What greater opportunity or calling is there than leading people to become acquainted with the Bible, the Word of God? This knowledge leads to a personal experience with the Lord Jesus, the one who inspired the pages of the Book of Life, the Bible. Sometimes, however, we seem to take for granted reaching people for Bible study. Then we are like an insurance salesman who lived on his renewals, when all around lived thousands of people without the adequate protection one of his company's policies would afford.

2. Enthusiasm comes from a knowledge of the materials with which you work. A close friend of mine works on his family genealogical tree in his spare time. He has little time to spare, but it's interesting to hear him talk when he's spent a day or two on his hobby. He goes to places most of us avoid–cemeteries, county courthouses, libraries, and archives. But ask him just one question and you set him off. He'll talk on and on. And the funny thing about it–his enthusiasm makes a dull subject sparkle and glow. Enthusiasm does it. He's enthusiastic because he's talking about something he knows plenty about.

Persons going through the Dale Carnegie Course often are amazed at the vigor shown by leaders of the course. Later they learn these men are thoroughly familiar with the work they do. This familiarity, in part, comes from the times they have repeated it, but in greater part from having learned so well the lessons it teaches. This thorough knowledge fosters a tremendous enthusiasm.

Southern Baptists know more about building Bible teaching programs than any other people. While many others have been signally blessed of God in the development of their Bible study approaches and programs, no other group has been able to enroll as many people over as wide a territory as have Southern Baptists. The history of the Southern Baptist Bible study program is one of almost continuous, unbroken growth. With the exception of the sixties and the years of World War I and World War II, every year for nearly 100 years has shown significant gains. If Southern Baptists have a genius, if they know any one thing above all others, it is how to grow Sunday Schools. That knowledge produces enthusiasm.

Although ACTION is new, the knowledge of how to use it to reach large numbers of people is readily available. That knowledge alone contributes to enthusiasm for reaching people. We know how; let us get on with the task.

3. Hearing testimonies of what is happening produces enthusiasm. And what great things are happening in these days! Every day's mail or news brings in new stories of what one church or what many churches have done. Such as the First Baptist Church of Gulfport, Mississippi, which enrolled nearly 300 new people in a week's time. And the First Baptist Church of Screven, Georgia, which enrolled eighty-two new people in a week's time and increased from 192 to 274 people enrolled in Sunday School. And Edinburg Baptist Church of Trenton, Missouri, which averaged 112 persons in Sunday School attendance, but in the month following an ACTION campaign averaged 173 with a high attendance on a special day of 238 persons. Stories like those cause those who hear them to become excited. They make a Christian want to become involved. They create enthusiasm.

4. *Success breeds enthusiasm.* Success follows when one takes the plan and follows it closely. Then as new people are reached, enthusiasm mounts. Of course, this is true in every area of church life, not in ACTION alone.

5. *Enthusiasm grows as one demonstrates enthusiasm.* Those who act enthusiastic become enthusiastic. Say something good. Tell something exciting. Feel an inner excitement at the prospect of what God is about to do in your life, in your church. When you feel this inner excitement, you find it easy to express what you feel. You may not say it with the best and choicest words, but what you feel communicates itself, nevertheless. Excitement is contagious. Enthusiasm is catching. As you express your own, the people of your church see it, feel it, understand it, taste it, and unconsciously–or consciously–begin to share it and communicate it to still others.

There is a place in everything we do for Christ to show a holy and joyous enthusiasm. It's easy to have this kind of feeling when the kind of things happen as described by Jim Thomas of the First Baptist Church in Groveport, Ohio.

> "This morning I had twenty-two people accept Jesus as their Savior and Lord at the morning service of my church, and I wondered what reason I could give for this happening. I knew. It was because of the ACTION program in our church. Two of those who were saved told me they'd never been inside a church before, but because someone came to their door the previous week and invited them to come and study the

Bible, they came. God got a chance at them during the Sunday School hour, for they had an excellent teacher who was alert to the opportunity afforded by their presence. Then I was able to present the gospel to them at the worship hour. Others of the twenty-two people who responded gave similar testimonies. Praise the Lord for his wonderful works."

From Fantastic Dream to Glorious Achievement

And the Spirit entered into me and set me on my feet (Ezek. 2:2, TLB).

The road to glorious achievement begins with a fantastic dream. The dream or vision begins to take shape and form when you are inspired to take some action, to make some effort.

How will your fantastic dream come to shape and form? As you think of the answers to the five questions below let the Holy Spirit lead your thoughts.

- What does your fantastic dream mean to you?
- How does the prospect of a fantastic growth in your Sunday School challenge you?
- Can your dream come to reality?
- What will God lead you to do to bring it to reality?
- When will you start?

Crystallize your thoughts by writing answers in the space below.

12. Share Your New Light

J. N. Barnette in his book *One to Eight* concluded that a church which enrolled 125 people for every 100 church members would baptize in a year one person for each eight members. He based this statement on a study made of a sizable amount of churches which were baptizing large numbers of people, along with a study of a group of churches baptizing relatively few in ratio to church membership. His idea, however, scarcely needed proof.

A church with a Sunday School enrollment larger by one-fourth than its church membership had under the influence of Bible teaching and gospel proclamation one person for every four church members—perhaps more. If it could win to Christ as many as half of these evangelistic prospects, its ratio of baptisms would be one to eight church members. His principle, that some of these prospects surely could be won, is as valid today as it was when first stated.

A matter of simple arithmetic tells you that enrolling people in Bible study increases the evangelistic thrust or opportunity of a church. A church with 100 members and 100 or less enrolled in its Bible study program is ministering largely to its own people. Almost the only unsaved people it's touching are the children of its committed families.

Is this wholly an imaginary church? No! As a matter

of fact, a majority of our churches have far fewer enrolled in their Sunday Schools than they have members. The statistics of the Southern Baptist Convention show the following: more than 12,000,000 members of churches, less than 8,000,000 enrolled in Sunday Schools. A study of individual churches shows the same sobering figures, as it must. Such a study could be made by a random sampling of churches and would come out similar to the following.

One church has in excess of 4,000 members. It has just above 2,000 enrolled in its Sunday School. Its ratio of baptisms? How could it be other than disappointing?

Another church has approximately 2,200 members. It has just above 1,200 enrolled in its Bible study program. Yet another church has 750 names on its church roll but scarcely 200 on its Sunday School roll. Another church with 100 members has enrolled only sixty in Bible study. One conclusion, quickly drawn, is that in all these churches, most of those enrolled in Sunday Schools, if not all, already are members of the church itself, or else they are the small children of present church members.

What effect does this condition have on the evangelistic thrust of a church? It limits it drastically. As the children of its families come to an age of decision, a large church may reach and baptize them and make a somewhat creditable showing, while never reaching a single person outside the circle of its own families.

But is that what Jesus meant when he spoke of his people going into all the world with the gospel proclamation? What about the wholly untouched. Is that the spirit of the Ephesian church of which was said, "All the people who lived in the province of Asia, both Jews and Gentiles, heard the word of the Lord" (Acts 19:10, TEV). To the same point: is that a modern-day version of the passion for souls that made Southern Baptists a great people of God?

These churches and all of our churches as a representative part need to break out into their surrounding communities in outreach for the unreached. This must be done through the use of our Sunday Schools as reaching tools.

Let's see how. A church uses ACTION to change its enrollment figures. Now the church with 100 members has 200 enrolled in its Sunday School. The church with 750 members and 200 enrolled in Sunday School uses ACTION both to enroll more of its church members and many unsaved people. Its enrollment increases from 200 to 350; while it still has fewer enrolled in Bible study than it has members, it does have many more people to touch for Christ. After using ACTION several times, it begins to balance church membership and Bible study enrollment. The large church must work harder to reach more people; perhaps it has more complacency to overcome. The actual numbers of people reached will be larger, however, and the satisfaction of reaching people will be rewarding.

But now that these people are enrolled in Bible study, how will the church proceed? How will it assure that there is a witness to those whom it enrolls? Several suggestions can be made.

1. The church must be led to accept, as part of its task and opportunity, witnessing to these people and winning them to faith in Christ. The pastor, the Sunday School director, and the Sunday School outreach director are the ones who must assume the lead in guiding the church to

do this. The pastor's class often helps a pastor lead his church in this direction.

Waylon B. Moore is the pastor of Spencer Memorial Baptist Church of Tampa, Florida. In a letter he describes how the church responded evangelistically as a result of an ACTION campaign.

> "I'm excited about the news of the growing ACTION emphasis. We have had people join five out of the last six Sundays through the ACTION ministry. I know of over twenty that were reached exclusively through ACTION that have joined, and most of the people in my class that have come have joined.
>
> "Suddenly I feel 'released' to enroll people all the time during the week. There is a freedom like flying involved in this ministry. Most of us as pastors simply wait until the next campaign or the next revival, hoping to grab a few more, and in between seem to settle down with what we have. I'm discovering I have to keep thinking of enrollment, and I'm not trained that way yet, but I'm getting convicted by the Spirit when a person joins I could have enrolled long before they joined, and they possibly would have joined sooner. Also, I am under the tremendous weight of trying to get enrollment thinking into the minds of our people. To me this is one of the great needs. How do we get people thinking enroll . . . enroll . . . enroll? I know it has to begin with me.
>
> "The pastor's class has been a smashing suc-

cess. I've not had over twenty-four, I believe, any week. We're moving toward our first social, and so many of the people in the class are brand new Christians, lost, or unchurched; it's a constant challenge. I've got an interesting class with a doctor, CPA, electrician, stone mason, concrete pourer, plus a bunch of widows, divorcees, lonely women whose husbands aren't interested. What a thrilling opportunity!"

2. Enlist workers to witness and win. When a Sunday School worker is enlisted and given a job description, he should have included a statement that he is to be a personal soul-winner. His first responsibility will be to witness to those who may be lost and enrolled in his class.

3. Develop workers to witness and win. This may be done through a regular training program in soul winning. The Lay Evangelism School is a tool for this, but a church may want to go beyond this either with a repeat of the Lay Evangelism School, or with specific training in the use of the Bible in soul-winning. Every Sunday School worker should be expected to receive the training. This actually equips the workers to witness to unsaved class members.

4. Prepare lists of persons who are evangelistic prospects. A technique for doing this is detailed in *Outreach Evangelism Through the Sunday School* by R. Othal Feather. This description may be followed, or the Sunday School outreach director may simply go through the department and class enrollment and record books making a list of all who are unsaved and unreached for church

membership. At one of the regular weekly workers' planning meetings speak of these responsibility lists and distribute them. Ask that teachers and other workers make a week-by-week effort to reach as many of these as possible.

5. Make a special effort during a revival season. When the church revival comes, lead all classes to seek out and witness to every class member who is unsaved or who is not a member of the individual church.

6. Make a continuing emphasis on evangelism. Evangelism through the Sunday School does not depend upon revival seasons, although they may help considerably. With unsaved people in the classes and departments the evangelism thrust may be a week-by-week continuing emphasis.

Does this work for a church? The answer is yes.

Lonnie Earnest of the First Baptist Church of Sebring, Florida, gives these statistics from his church. During the months of October, November, and December, 1974, the average attendance was 413. In October the following year the church engaged in ACTION, enrolling 388 people and increasing attendance approximately 100. In 1974 the church received for baptism and baptized nine people during the three-month period. Following ACTION in October, 1975, the church baptized forty-two people during that month, November, and December. The year before ACTION, the church had received five people on transfer of membership. After ACTION they received sixty by letter in the same period of time. What made the difference between fourteen members one year and 102 in the same time frame the following year? ACTION!

It will do the same for any church that witnesses to

people being enrolled. Don't wait. Follow the example of pastor Ted Burrell, who wrote:

> "Thanks for the excellent job you did in leading our ACTION program. We had 597 in Sunday School this past week. Tuesday we began our personal witness training and sharing Christ with the lost. Presently twenty people are involved. Please continue to pray for us."

The early day Separate Baptists often called themselves "New Lights." They believed the coming of Jesus Christ into their lives was like the shining of a new light. It illuminated and transformed them and was a light shining along their pathway. They believed that after seeing and experiencing this new light for themselves they should share it with all others. This is what witnessing to those we enroll means: sharing our new light with them.

13.
Let Your Children Walk Alone

I must open this chapter by relating a precious story. One Sunday morning following Sunday School, a lady dropped by to pick up her child. On her way home she was questioning the child, who was about five years of age, concerning what she learned that day in Sunday School. And the talkative child said, "Well, mother, we learned today a song about Brother Andy."

"What do you mean? We love Brother Andy. But we don't sing about him," the mother said.

The child answered, "Yes, we did today."

The mother said, "Well, sweetheart, I think you must be mistaken, because we really don't ever sing about Brother Andy, though we love him so very very much."

"Mommy, we did today."

"Sweetheart, how did the song go?"

And the little child sang, "Andy walks with me, Andy talks with me."!!!

The story means a great deal to me. I was delighted that a little child would even consider the fact that I, as her pastor, would walk with her and talk with her. But the story carries far beyond that. I hope and pray that my almost thirty years in the pastorate produced far more than that. I hope it produced some of my spiritual children, knowing that I walked with them and talked with them also.

It was a rich experience in helping my babes in Christ learn to walk and talk with Jesus, and then see them discipled into *disciplers.* When I was thinking about this subject, I was keying in on my own personal life. My introduction into denominational work came when first and foremost the Spirit of God touched my life and led me to the place where he wanted me to serve at this particular time. And when Dr. Grady Cothen and Dr. A. V. Washburn opened the door, invited me to join them in reaching the United States for Christ, they trusted me and released me to do the work God had called me to do. Jesus trusts us to do his work.

And, of course, we must trust others. I could not do all that was required of me. As the ACTION program began to develop, so many requests came to my desk. I was only one man, but I could send out others to lead in ACTION, too. So one by one men were selected, trained, and released. And I would like to write about two of these men who have probably conducted more ACTION programs than any other persons on earth at this particular time.

"I count it a privilege to have been able to have a part in such a wonderful thing as ACTION," says Dr. Bob Anderson, as he tells his story. Dr. Anderson is a dentist, a deacon, and the Sunday School director of Riverside church.

"Few people are granted in a lifetime the opportunity to share in anything which has such a profound effect on the lives of so many.

"As we worked in the ACTION program, I became

acutely aware of the vast number of lost people everywhere about us. I also realized that we must do something to reach them. In ACTION we discovered we had a tool that could be used by the average church member. We also found out that by combining the ACTION program with a liberal dose of concern and enthusiasm we could see lost people saved. To this end we dedicated ourselves as we traveled from church to church leading churches to reach some of these spiritually needy people.

"I began to have an increasing burden for the lost as we continued to go from place to place. I began to feel that I might be called to full-time Christian work. I found, after a time, that I could no longer exhort people to do something I myself was not totally involved in. Yet, I knew God had given me a special skill as a dentist and that I was going to give it back to him."

"Certainly ACTION has affected my life," Frank Land says. "I know that when ACTION presents an opportunity for me to go, I simply cannot say no. Nor do I want to say no. I know when I am in another community working the Lord Jesus in my own way, which I wish were more effective, that my wife and children are at home holding me up in prayer. Even though I am gone many weekends leading ACTION campaigns in churches, the personal life of my family has become a sweeter-than-ever experience. God has done fantastic things for me and for my family.

"One of my favorite illustrations is one shared with me by Roland Davis who said he wasn't going to 'another one of them there seminars' until he checked out the guy doing the leading to smell whether he had smoke on his clothes. I like to tell the people where I go that I have walked through the fire of ACTION, and I've got smoke on my clothes–please come and join me. In fact, when I was in Jackson, Mississippi, one of the consultants from the Baptist Sunday School Board, who was there to see and observe, said he wanted to go out with the Task Force. 'I can't stand and say I've got smoke on my clothes unless I go out with the Task Force,' he said. I'm like him; I'm able to say that I've been there."

Bob Anderson and Frank Land are two men who do have "smoke on their clothes." Praise the Lord for them and for the dozens of others I knew in Riverside who became involved. Praise the Lord for the multiplied dozens of others I'm coming to know all across the nation, as more and more people are involved in reaching more people for the glory of Christ. Praise the Lord for the ones in your churches you'll help to get "smoke on their clothes."

14.
Get Away From Your Own Front Door

After Riverside Church had engaged in ACTION several times, we knew we were reaching more of the people on our church field than we had ever dreamed possible. Enthusiasm and excitement ran at flood tide, and the happiness of the church matched these. Yet, we became increasingly conscious–and concerned–that there were many people so distant from us that we had little, if any, real expectation of reaching them. Some may not have been too far from Riverside to attend, but they thought they were. Others really were so far away we could not expect them to attend. What could we do for these?

"We need to get away from our own front door," someone said to me one day. That was the answer–get away from our own front door. How could we do it?

We began with a study, determined first to pinpoint sections of our county, Lee County, which needed new Sunday Schools and preaching services. Soon we had identified four of these. We decided to create a Sunday School in each section, four new Sunday Schools.

Our major hurdle was money; we had none. We'd spent all we had and more trying to provide necessary facilities at Riverside, the home base. However, we felt we had to go ahead. We wanted to reach these people.

Folks in these communities were without Christ, some were dying weekly, and we were not witnessing to them. Determined to do something, we developed an idea, a plan.

First, we would locate a building in each of the areas, one we could rent free or for a very small charge. Soon we found these. One was a building which had been used by NASA as a tracking station. Now closed, the building was one we were able to secure without cost. The second building we discovered was a county-owned structure, a community building we could secure also without cost. For the third meeting place we found a recreation building in a large mobile home park. In one area, the fourth, we were unable to locate a building. However, there we found two families, each of whom owned a double-width trailer with their living rooms facing each other across a narrow roadway. Some of our buildings were larger, some were smaller, but in any circumstance we had four places in which to begin our work, *and we'd spent no money.*

I was ready for the second step. I found four preachers, men who were ordained and qualified to lead the work. I told these men in the beginning that all I could promise them was a place to preach. I could give them no pay other than a place to proclaim the gospel of Jesus Christ. They wanted this and accepted gladly.

The third step might be more difficult. What would I do for beginning leadership? I prayed, and God gave me my answer. I found four deacons not then on the active fellowship and asked them if they would serve as Sunday School directors in the four missions. Each one agreed. I was pleased; this gave needed doctrinal security. I suppose if we can't find that in four "good old deacons," we can't find it anywhere.

I instructed these men for their task and asked them to select from our membership the workers they needed for their new Sunday School organizations. Each one required no more than five to ten workers with which to begin. I asked them not to raid our present Sunday School organization. Because they knew the membership of our church, they were able to make their selections and enlist their workers.

Next, we laid out the geographical area each new Sunday School would reach. And selected four Task Forces. These were brought together on a given Sunday, and while we had lunch together, I trained them. I asked them to enroll as many as possible but not to exceed the number needed to give us a capacity crowd. We thought that approximately 40 percent of the people we enrolled would attend from the very beginning. If we had room for forty people to attend, we knew we should not enroll more than approximately 100. These four Task Forces left the church and went out to enroll people.

Did this plan succeed? Look at how well it succeeded. On the next Sunday morning four new Sunday Schools and morning worship services were established simultaneously with maximum attendances–an average of sixty persons present per Sunday School.

This project had not cost us a cent. We received literature for the four from the Sunday School Department of The Baptist Sunday School Board without cost for the first quarter. The Sunday School Department regularly makes this provision for new Sunday Schools. New hymn books also were given us by The Sunday School Board. Therefore, at the time of the first Sunday, we had expended hardly a cent.

The offerings from these four missions was placed in four bank accounts and permitted to increase, so when they were able to build, there would be monies for them.

Let me share with you one further chapter in this story. First, the new Sunday School established in the ex-NASA tracking station had to be closed because the owner spread liquid fertilizer around the building each Saturday and made it impossible for us to remain in the building on Sunday. Whether or not this was intentional does not really matter, but this was the circumstance. We could not continue that Sunday School. However, we secured property in that area, and worked up plans to begin a second time.

A second Sunday School felt that it was best for them to unite with an existing Southern Baptist Church in their area, and almost all the people who had been enrolled, transferred there. We did not feel we lost ground in this situation.

The other two new Sunday Schools continued to grow. Property was secured, and a building was soon constructed on one site, while plans got underway for the other. These new units have never drawn from the financial resources of the mother church. And it was my personal conviction as the pastor of the church at that time that we could have established ten new Sunday Schools without adversely affecting our own church, if ten had been needed. In fact, the mission spirit of our church grew more intense because of these new Sunday Schools.

This is not an untried idea. Al Dawson who is a director of associational missions in South Florida related to me recently that it had been his privilege to establish nineteen Southern Baptist Churches. In each case he located a meeting place, sought and enlisted a small corps of leaders, and went into the community to enroll people in a Sunday School, which at the time did not exist. All of these new Sunday Schools are in existence today–all have become churches. Some are among the largest churches in the state of Florida. He merely went to communities ripe for a new Sunday School and church and personally enrolled people for the new Sunday School. They remained for church, and so the new work began.

This was so thrilling for us because we did not have to struggle with only a handful. We began with a capacity attendance in every place. How many people in our nation are not in Bible study? How many communities do not have a Sunday School or an evangelistic preaching service? These people and communities are waiting for Southern Baptists to come to them, and we must go. I wish it were possible to give credit to all the people who provided these new missions in our own church. One of our deacons, Albert Miller, was chairman of the missions committee when all of this took place. This man has been one of the most faithful Christian gentlemen and outreach leaders ever known. Albert guided these new missions from their inception and is still serving in this capacity today.

The two mission pastors who have continued to work, Gene Highfill and Ray Gould, certainly ought to be remembered as men willing to go and do a job without remuneration. Because their hearts were on fire for mission work, they accepted calls to these positions. Albert Miller, Milton DeSear, Jerry Skinner, and Kerry Forkey were the four men who were Sunday School directors. These men were willing by faith to begin with nothing and build a Sunday School in an unusually unique way. They certainly are men who have set the pace for Southern Baptists today. I wish it were possible for every reader to visit these missions and look in on the work that is being done and see the dedicated men and women who work at the side of these leaders in order to get the job done.

Getting beyond the front door of the church can be done in another way. Let me tell you about Lillie King, a member of the First Baptist Church of Cheraw, South Carolina. She had never been enrolled in the Bible study program of the church for, you see, Lillie was an amputee. She had lost a leg and was confined to a wheel chair in a nursing home. Some of the people visited the nursing home and told Lillie about what her church was doing: enrolling people in Bible study wherever they found them. "I'm not enrolled," said Lillie. "But I'd like to be."

After being enrolled, Lillie still didn't know how she'd attend. But she thought the church might provide some kind of Bible study for her. If for her, then why not for all those living in her nursing home? She asked for enough enrollment cards for all these. In the next few days she went from room to room and enrolled every person in the home. The following Sunday morning, the church sent workers to organize an adult department away from the church building. The meeting place overflowed into the halls!

15.
Lead an ACTION Revival

During my ministry I have participated in about 200 revival meetings. Some of these were times when the Spirit of God was evidenced by the work he did. Others I fear were just "protracted meetings" which were conducted because the church calendar called for them.

I believe that most of us pray for the Holy Spirit of God to take charge. This is why we design certain types of prayer meetings into our plans, and every kind of blessing has come through this route. Surely we should pray as though everything depended upon God, but should participate as though everything depended on us.

In these meetings, whether in my own church or in others, one of my most discouraging activities was trying to induce my people to properly prepare for and participate in these efforts. They wanted the best evangelists and musicians, but the prayer periods were not always well-attended and even worse were often lacking in genuine concern, confession, and compassion. I varied our approach to most of our meetings in the hope that variety would entice participation.

Three years ago when I began to use the ACTION enrollment program, I felt led to use it in connection with a revival and uncover a new key to success in seeing human participation. Let me share with you how it has developed.

On the first Sunday I used the regular ACTION plan which is a plan designed to get my people committed to a definite participation. During the Sunday School I explained a little to them about the philosophy of the open enrollment. At the morning worship service, I shared with them even more. Then on Sunday afternoon the Task Force actually participated in the plan. Finally, on Sunday evening the rest of my people were committed to spiritual activity.

Monday through Saturday was given to a regular revival meeting. We had morning services. These services were thirty minutes in length at the church from 10:00 to 10:30. And then from 10:30 until noon those involved in the morning segment of the Task Force went out and knocked on doors to enroll people. The Task Force returned at noon for a time of testimony and prayer.

Then, in the evening beginning about 5:00 or 5:30 the evening section of the Task Force went visiting. Those involved in the telephone committee did their telephoning, and our youth came in order to make visits.

What we discovered was that these people did go and return to the church around 7:30 in time for the evening worship service. We discovered some other facts. I had been trying to encourage my people to visit. What I discovered was that when they were actively involved in ACTION, they made *about 150 calls per couple per week,* and this enabled us to reach a huge segment of our city.

The Task Force members first and foremost were trying to enroll people in Bible study, but before they left the homes they visited, they shared with the people that a revival meeting was being conducted at the church. The

Task Force members gave them a flier with an invitation to attend. This enabled us to get the needed visits made.

Second, the people doing the telephoning, after they had tried to enroll people in Sunday School, shared news about the revival. So did the young people, and so did the pastor when he enrolled for the pastor's class and those working in the bus ministry. So, thousands of visits were made, and every one of those had in them an element of revival visitation.

Third, I encouraged my people to pray. But it was extremely difficult to put the burden on their hearts. However, when they made these contacts they saw the actual circumstances that existed in our community, many of them for the first time. They saw alcoholics. They saw prostitutes. They saw people with all types of sinful lives. Usually when our visitors came back to the church, they were so burdened they would get by themselves in small groups and pray.

So, when we gathered together in the evening for the revival, we had the services bathed in prayer. We had an interest and a concern that we had never known before. We had a much larger attendance because of the visitation and invitations that had been extended. We had more people saved because more lost people were present, and we were able to give our evangelist a larger love offering because we had more people there.

During the week of revival we continued to enroll and encourage people to be present on the following Sunday. We discovered that when the revival was over we had an enrollment far larger than ever before and an attendance which was a record-breaker. But in addition to that, the attendance never did sag. It continued high because it was a result of enrollment rather than gimmicky promotion.

What kind of results does this type of revival produce? The following letter from Tommy E. Lovorn, pastor, First Baptist Church, Cheraw, South Carolina, answers the question as well or better than I could.

May 26, 1975

Rev. E. S. Anderson
P. O. Box 818
Fort Myers, Florida 33902

Dear Andy,

I have written you previously expressing our appreciation for a job well done in leading our ACTION Sunday School Revival April 27 through May 2, 1975. At that time, I promised you a follow-up letter in a few weeks, indicating our statistics. Here goes:

Our Sunday School report for March shows an enrollment of 562 with an average attendance of 370. After the six-day ACTION Revival (Sunday through Friday), our Sunday School enrollment was 1,002. This is a net gain of 440. I am happy to report that attendance for the past four Sundays following the campaign has been around the 550 mark. We have continued the follow-up plan and now have leveled off our enrollment after four weeks at 700.

I am thoroughly enjoying my Pastor's Class which had an initial enrollment of eighty-five with forty-five attending the first Sunday. We have leveled off now at about thirty-five. These are people who would not be in Sunday School if it were not for this class. I am thoroughly enjoying my contact with these people and our study of prophecy together.

Andy, as your hometown church, we are proud that you were able to personally come and lead us in this revolutionary new Sunday School approach. Thanks for letting us be in on the ground floor. I can predict that ACTION will make it big! It has certainly been an inspiration to our people. It has given us a shot in the arm and a boost when things were lagging. Not only did the campaign cause a real revival among our people, but it got them to moving, visiting, and witnessing when they thought they could not. It has resulted in packed crowds every Sunday with chairs down the aisles. On the first Sunday, we initiated a drive-in church without realizing we had done so. Because the church was filled to overflowing, latecomers had to sit in their cars and listen to the service over their car radios. The whole town is talking about what is happening at First Baptist Church.

Although not everyone we enrolled has followed through with their commitment, it still has given us a list of new prospects to continue to work on. We are continuing our entire church visitation program through the Sunday School as a result of ACTION. We hope to repeat the campaign later and achieve even greater results. Thank you for bringing it our way.

In His love,

Tommy E. Lovorn
Pastor

Speaking as an evangelistic pastor-consultant, I personally do not believe I will ever conduct another revival meeting which is not an ACTION revival. For I believe we accomplish far more permanent good in this type of revival than in any other that I personally have been involved with.

The purpose of everything that a church does ultimately is to help men know Jesus Christ. We can reach people through Jesus Christ as we have never before reached them. And when we do, we will win more to Christ than we have ever won. One of the greatest benefits coming from this type of evangelism is that: across the years when we have led someone to Christ in their home, business, or on the street, it has been difficult for us to get them into the church for discipleship. We lost a great number of them, but when we enrolled them in Sunday School and they were won to Christ as a result of God speaking through his Word, they were already in the church, and so conservation was almost 100 percent. I believe we ought to further the evangelistic emphasis of our churches by sharing our Sunday School organizations and teaching.

16.
Stop to Look at Yourself

Evaluation is not a word Southern Baptists love. But the church which I pastored and I myself profited by stopping long enough to look at ourselves. Let me tell you a very intimate—and warm—experience. It has never been put into print, and perhaps some people will not understand it. As I share it with you, remember that it is a part of my very being, an innermost part, that I am baring to you.

After sixteen years as pastor of Riverside, I recognized the church was beginning to lose its momentum and beginning to decrease. Nothing serious, but it was just not growing. This was a disturbing factor for me, so much so that I didn't know which way to turn. Having been success-oriented across the years, I felt that I could "do it by myself," but everything I tried seemed to backfire.

There was no great unrest in the church, but there certainly was a divine discontent within my heart. I had been stopped by the Lord. And forced to look long and hard at myself. I suppose I took some self-pride in the fact that I had a regular devotional life each morning and spent considerable time in studying God's Word and preparing my own heart and life as I worked up the messages for the people I loved. But there was still a longing within me. Now, as I look back on it, it seems as if these things came to pass in order for me to get squared away—to search my soul.

For some unknown reason I had never been impressed with the subject of fasting. But all of a sudden, the subject consumed me. I had no idea of how to study it. Of course, I had mentioned it in my sermons across the years, but never with any deep interest or concern. So, my first impression was, "I wonder if there is somebody who fasts that I can talk to?" I began to look. The only people I could find were those of a century or more ago—men like Finney, Sankey, and Whitefield. But they were gone to be with the Lord.

I couldn't find a person who fasted as a way of life. I have found some since, however, but at the time I couldn't find any. I decided to find a good book on the subject. I found only two in print, and both of these were written from a sensational standpoint. I still couldn't discover what I wanted. I suppose the Lord was closing all of the doors and forcing me back to the Scriptures, where I belonged, anyway.

I read the Bible from Genesis to Revelation in search for every passage on the subject of fasting. I pulled these out and made an exegetical study of them. And I have never seen so much that I had totally overlooked. Once I had digested this material the best I could, I decided the best thing for me to do was experiment. I did not know how to fast. I did not know what to leave off. What to eat or drink? Whether to eat or drink anything? And if so, how much? I did not realize how long a person could stay on a fast, although I found three supernatural fasts in the Bible. I found where others fasted for great lengths of time, and yet some fasted for short periods of time. I discovered that people were naturally hungry after fasts, but I didn't know if I could go one day without passing out without food!

So I decided that my first fast would be at home, so if I did pass out there would be somebody there to take care of me! This shows you just how ignorant I was. I did not understand why I was fasting–or what would be accomplished by fasting, but I knew there was a hunger in my heart that was beyond anything I had ever witnessed before. Surely God had stopped me in my tracks as a learning experience.

One of the major discoveries concerning fasting was this: it was not a way to get something from God by paying penance. It was not twisting the arm of God, but it was a time during which I emptied myself of food, but also emptied myself of sin and self-reliance. During most of my confession sessions in prayer, I had spent very little time digging out the sins of my life. But when I began to fast, I realized I was to concentrate on the garbage in my life. And oh, what I found! It was fearful. I did not realize there was so much that displeased God, but it was only after I took sufficient time fasting and confessing that God was able to begin to bless my life.

Through this experience I had a cleansing which I had never before experienced. And with that cleanness came the presence of God such as I had never known in the past. My prayer life turned into a thing of beauty. My personal relationship with God was enhanced beyond anything I had ever known. And it seemed that God spoke personally to me. It was during this time when I was quiet before God that he was able, not only to help me look at myself as he looks at me, but to give me some of the thoughts he had been wanting to share with me for many years. And I had been too busy to listen. For twenty-six years, the first twenty-six years of my ministry, there had been some element of success in the church growth each year. This satisfied me from one standpoint, and yet I was dissatisfied because I was experiencing virtual failure. Now I was able to see and witness and understand the mind of God with a newness.

It was through these experiences that I feel God was able to share so much with me during the last three years. During the time that I have practiced fasting in my own personal life, I believe God has dealt with me more deeply. I feel that there has been a personal growth exceeding any three years of my life.

It does pay to stop and look at yourself. This is not only true of an individual, but also of a church. We knew that we were at a standstill, and when we stopped to pray, things happened, things that defy the imagination. For we grew more in one month than we had grown in the previous sixteen years! This indicates something of God's willingness to bless us once we have paid the price of examining ourselves, confessing our sins, and committing ourselves totally to God.

God may reveal himself to you in another approach; he may cause you to stop in another way. But if you are restless and yearning–at the same time pining to do his will–he will give you the opportunity of seeing yourself, your church, and the condition of the community.

17.
Spark the Fire of Ambition

"Andy, you're a self-starter," someone said to me. "Can you tell us what it is that makes you that kind of person?"

At the time I was not sure what was meant by the expression, so I decided to put together some ideas that might help motivate someone to give his best for Christ.

Perhaps the *benefits* a person might receive would motivate him to action. That's a strong motivating factor in selling anything. Even a denominational program is sold to pastors and church leaders on the basis of what benefit the church receives from it.

The opening pages of the widely distributed *Reach Out Manual* for 1974 furnished an example of how that could be done. These pages presented dramatically some of the benefits that could come to the church that followed the *Reach Out plan.* Among these were: the discovery of a large number of prospects, an enrollment increase, an attendance increase, and a possible record-breaking attendance on High Attendance Day, Pastors and churches wanted these benefits—and they received them from *Reach Out.*

That's one of the reasons ACTION has been widely accepted by pastors and churches. It promises one thing:

an increase in Sunday School enrollment. And it delivers that promise when a church and pastor use the ACTION manual and follow closely the suggested pattern of preparation.

But I thought my "spark" was more than that, even if I admitted it was that. I thought of what I call my "Arabia." I don't tell it often, but I want to tell it here.

The highway was lonely for it was late at night. Patches of fog could be seen in the low places. The green light from the instrument panel made our faces look ghostly as the car moved almost silently through the night.

The four of us were talking about a new mission church when Earl Southerland cried, "Albert." Our attention was drawn to a semi-trailer truck which was barreling down upon us. Only a short second ticked from the time I looked up into the grill of that giant vehicle until it struck the car broadside, in the door where I was sitting.

Sound and smell and pain erupted like a volcano. Amid the breaking of glass; the bending, tearing and ripping of steel; the squeal of tires as they squirmed sideways across the highway; the smell of burning rubber, of oil, gas and dust; the groan and cry of pain burst from our lungs as chaos ruled. I remember it all, for I was there.

The car broke loose from the truck and came to a rocking standstill. The right rear door had been crushed in over my legs. The side of the car was completely demolished. My body was prostrate across the seat. Even though I was conscious, I was unable to breathe–probably, my lungs had collapsed. I tried to sit up, I struggled for breath. I sucked for air, but none came. I panicked as self-preservation took control. I could not speak since I had no breath. I could not call for help or express my predicament. I fought for life.

I suppose I had shown compassion for those who suffer with tuberculosis, emphysema or other related respiratory diseases, but not until this experience did I know what it was to starve for air.

Breath would not return. I knew the end of life had arrived. In a panic calmness I prayed, "Lord, here I am. I want to stay on earth but take me if you wish." How many times had I wondered what my reaction would be when it came time to die. I discovered the answer that night, January 4, 1968. The Christian has nothing to fear in death.

I beat upon my chest and struggled for air—it came. I do not know why it came, but it did. My life was spared.

The chairman of our deacons, Howard Devore, was sitting in the rear seat with me. He discovered that I had a hard head for, in the impact, it was driven into his side. I recall that he was the first person to speak. He knew I was alive, for he had seen my thrashing around, so he called to Earl and Albert Miller, the driver, who were in the front seat. They answered. Both were injured but alive. Blood was everywhere. The black silence was broken only by the groans of pain. None of us realized the extent of our injuries, but I knew my leg was broken and my shoulder crushed.

Within minutes the ambulance arrived. The attendants, using their radio, alerted the sheriff's department, who sent a deputy to inform my family. At the hospital, I found more friends—many of them—each desiring to help. In the midst of the organized turmoil of nurses, doctors, X-ray technicians, and police officers, they brought a man to my stretcher who introduced himself as the driver of the truck. He expressed his sorrow that the accident had taken place. After talking with him for a few moments, I asked if he were a Christian. He answered "No." I tried to explain to him the value of the Christian faith, but circumstances limited our talk. I learned that there is an opportunity to witness for Christ no matter where you are or what the circumstances may be.

I do not recall many of the events of the next twelve to fourteen days except the presence of my wife in my room. But the love of the people was overwhelming. They came with flowers, food, gifts, cards, letters, prayers and almost everything you can think of. So great was their generosity, we had to request that some of the things be discontinued.

Then came the days of convalescence.

Why did it happen? I wanted to know. I read the book of Galatians. When the apostle Paul became a Christian, he did not go to the other apostles for advice, but the Holy Spirit sent him to Arabia, to the desert, where he remained for three years—after which he returned with a fresh, warm message from God. Somehow, I feel that this was my trip into Arabia.

"Arabia" may be a desert for some, but for me it was an oasis. Years have passed since that night, two more visits into the operating room, months in bed, in a wheelchair, and on crutches, and at least one more surgery is planned. Discouraged? No! These have been the best years of my life. Why? Because I was living life so rapidly I had no time to enjoy it. Even though my wife and I had been happily married for more than twenty years, I did not really know her or our three children until this experience.

There were many things I had wanted to do, but there was never enough time. God gave me that time when he sent me to "Arabia." I had wanted to compose a home study New Testament Greek course for laymen and pastors who could not attend college, Bible school, or seminary. Many had expressed a longing to be able to read the New Testament in its original language. My wife placed my portable typewriter and my books on the bed tray so I could write when I felt strong enough. This course was completed and is presently being studied by laymen and pastors in almost every state in America and several foreign countries. One college has placed it in its curriculum. God sent me to "Arabia" to write it.

There never seemed to be enough time for prayer, but with other activities curtailed, time became available. Although our church had almost 1600 members, I prayed for each one every day (except on days when I was out of my study). Many things which I thought were important were replaced with things of more importance.

I'm glad God let me go to "Arabia."

A pastor friend of mine suffered a serious heart attack. As he thought of what had happened to him, he came to believe it would be better if he should resign. He didn't know what would happen to his family and how they would be cared for, but did write out a note to the chairman of deacons.

Later the deacon chairman came to him and told him several things. He personally refused to accept the resignation; he wanted his pastor to continue as his own pastor. He assured the pastor that the greatest days of the church and of his own ministry were ahead. He told the pastor that the church would move along while he recuperated and wanted the pastor to use the time of recuperation for rest and for planning what he most deeply desired to see the church accomplish. He also told the pastor that the deacons and other church members were making certain that the hospital bills were paid without creating an undue financial strain upon the pastor's financial resources.

The following day the doctors noticed a decided improvement in the patient's condition. The pastor used six weeks of recovery and another six weeks of limited activity to study and plan his ministry. The church entered into its greatest period of growth and development.

The point of the story is not that men may recover from heart attacks. Neither is the point that deacons may support their pastors in a time of need. Both of these applications are legitimate, but the point made here is that a person is motivated strongly by having an objective worth living for.

The objective of ACTION is increasing the number of people enrolled. It does act as a stimulant or a starter for many pastors. It should motivate every pastor—in fact, every one of us, whether pastor or layperson, who wants to serve Christ our Lord.

18. Reach for More than You Can Grasp

Robert Browning, the English poet, inspired this chapter title. It has been one of the most challenging statements in my life.

I have been goal-oriented most of my life. For instance, I had an educational goal. I had a date set for when I would finish my B.D. Another when I would finish my master's, and now I have a goal for the completion of my doctorate. I believe God expects us, especially those of us who are Christians, to have goals in life. He does not intend for us to drift through life aimlessly and lie down in bed at night and say, "Thank you, I am alive. Help me to get up and wander some more tomorrow." Oh, how much more could be accomplished if we only had goals and would strive to reach them!

I had goals for my church, and annually, semiannually, monthly, and weekly, we tried to reach these attainments. When we discovered the prospects of growth through ACTION, we began to increase our goals considerably, for we were able to reach far more people than we had ever dreamed possible. After we had attained several exciting goals, the people of our church felt they could reach the entire county for Jesus Christ. In fact, a banner was placed in the front of our balcony which read

"Win Lee County Now." I knew we could not do it, but I did not want to tell them they couldn't. And I did not want anyone else telling them they couldn't. When I figured it up, I discovered it would have taken a 125-acre lot to park the cars on. But when the people had this type of outreach vision, I wanted to go with them.

We organized, talked about it, prayed about it, and someone suggested that there was a possibility that we might be able to enroll 5,000 new people during a ten-day period of time. This, of course, was an unheard of figure. Though we did not enroll 5,000, we did enroll 1,300 new people during the ten-day period. I was delighted over the fact that our people set a goal and grasped for it. What would have happened if we had not had an aggressive goal of 5,000. If we had only reached for 1,300, we probably would not have received more than 1,000–maybe 500. Who knows?

But we need to increase our vision considerably over what it is now. I was thrilled some months ago when I directed an ACTION program in the First Baptist Church, Atlanta, Georgia. At the conclusion of the evening service, the people of that great church, under the leadership of Dr. Charles Stanley, said they would set a goal to enroll 3,629 new Sunday School members during this year. At the time of this writing it looks like they are just about halfway to that goal. This is the kind of vision we need–reaching for even more than we can grasp.

A few weeks ago I was in the Hoffmantown Baptist Church in Albuquerque, New Mexico, and under the direction of their pastor, Dr. James Bryant, this church decided that it would someday be the greatest Sunday School in the Southern Baptist Convention. Their immediate goal was to enroll 1,700 people in Bible study. Somehow I have a feeling that the leadership of that church will reach that goal.

In talking with Dr. W. A. Criswell, pastor of the First Baptist Church, Dallas, Texas, I was almost shocked out of my senses when I realized that the leadership of that church decided that they would reach *8,000* new people in Sunday School enrollment as soon as possible. For a church which seemingly has achieved almost anything any church could ever want, these folks realized that they must reach their community for Jesus Christ, and so they have reached for even more than they can grasp. Under the leadership of that great pastor, I am sure they will go far beyond even this initial goal. We need to think and plan for more and greater goals. For a church will not reach any further than it sees.

Without a vision the people perish. Personally speaking, I would like to see the day when our denomination and its various component parts would again set some outstanding goals for us to shoot at. For instance, I have three personal goals for the Southern Baptist Convention. These have never been approved by anyone. They are just goals that I personally would like to see attained. First, within the next ten years, I would like to see us increase our Sunday Schools and churches from 35,000 to 100,000. We need to reach America for Jesus Christ. We can never do it with 35,000 churches. It will take at least 100,000 units to do the job. I believe if we set that goal and go after it, we could achieve it within ten years. We need to bring lands under cultivation for the gathering of an increased production of people.

In our church at Ft. Myers we felt there was a need

for four new Sunday Schools and churches—church style missions, and one day we established these four with maximum attendance in each one without it costing us a cent. I believe that Southern Baptists could in one day establish 35,000 new Sunday Schools. If we could only see this vision, see the possibility, break our goal down for the denomination, to a state level, then to an associational level, then to individual church level, I believe this could be accomplished any time we decide we want to do the job. That's the first goal that I have for our denomination.

The second one is this.

It would be a thrill for us to set a goal to double the Sunday School enrollment within the next decade. That is going from 7,200,000 to 15,000,000. This would not be an impossibility. The broader the base from which we work—70,000 or 100,000 churches—this could easily be accomplished. It could be almost as easily accomplished by using the 35,000 Sunday Schools we presently have. If we could set a goal for 1,000,000 a year, and divide this goal to the state level, associational level, and church level, it would give our individual pastors and church leaders a church vision of what needs to be accomplished in order to reach the larger goal.

Third, I would like to see Southern Baptists set a goal to win to Christ and baptize a minimum of 1,000,000 people a year. We have seen the greatest number of baptisms of any denomination; however we have not begun to do what needs to be done. If we enroll 1,000,000 people a year, I believe we will come close to baptizing that many a year.

These are just the basics. But no goal will ever be successful as long as it is a general goal covering a whole denomination. This has to be broken down by segments. Daniel Burnham said, "Make no little plans. They have no magic to stir men's blood. Make big plans." We need to establish prayer-inspired faith goals. They must be specific. If we have nothing to aim at, we cannot achieve it. Remember nothing becomes dynamic until it becomes specific. When the goal becomes crystallized in our minds and hearts, then mountains can be moved.

What size church does Jesus need in your community? In setting the goal we must contact the Head of the church, Jesus Christ, and find out what he wants to have for a goal. Once we have listened to him, we must act responsibly. A faith goal leaps over non-growth excuses. It is more than using the past growth (or decline) of the school as a basis for this projection. That's arithmetic, not faith. "Will a faith goal work for me?" That's like asking if God is true to his promise. He promises to bless faith, and he does.

This is God's work. "Without faith it is impossible to please him" (Hebrews 11:6). The spiritual power of a faith goal can be the key which unlocks new doors of power and growth in your personal life and in the life of your church. While most of our goals are numerical, we must remember that numbers are only shorthand for people. *The goal is people.* People who need to know Jesus. We do not set quality against quantity. They must be as one. What about a faith goal to double your Sunday School enrollment this year?

How About You and Your Church?

I Challenge You

In an airport waiting room: his hair had a well-oiled look with an Elvis Presley sweep. His carry-on attache case and other paraphernalia gave me the impression he was an attorney. His suit was navy blue with an expensive-looking tie. When he looked up at his wife, I noticed something was wrong with his eyes. He couldn't focus them on her. She was very pretty, looked like a Southern belle. Her complexion was like a peach, with heavy rouge. She was expensively dressed. Only her ugly, modern-styled shoes took my eyes away.

A large 300-pound black woman sat in the next seat. She overflowed into the two seats which were next to her. Her hair was white. Her teeth and dress were white. She was contagiously happy. One reason was her twelve-year-old granddaughter was flying with her for the first time. I knew she was twelve because grandmother told all of us.

Next to these sat a middle-aged woman, who wore the kind of expression on her face that told me she was greatly troubled. Now and then she smiled with a quick, artificial change of expression, but only heaven knows what the heavy makeup covered. Her eyes were troubled, face drawn, and wrinkles permanently set. I wondered if anyone could ever break through and release the beauty God had originally created in her.

A man out of the fifties. I know that was his era because of his crew cut. But then one foot must be in the seventies because of his highheeled shoes. Green, white, and red plaid Scottish pants and turtle neck shirt. His face was open and clean looking. He reminded me of an independent Baptist preacher.

A blonde of about fifty–I should try to guess a woman's age!–sat next to him. Her posture was perfect. I saw her when she entered the compartment. She was nearly six feet tall, shoulders squared and walked stately. She was immaculately dressed, every blonde hair was in place, piled high on her head. She probably lived in a large mansion and had several servants. She rode first class. What a strange combination sat there across from me.

The next woman was in her early twenties. She came in with a younger girl. They must have been sisters. The younger girl flew with us, but the older didn't. I wondered about their background; they were crude and coarse. The older wore faded dungarees, a blouse with no bra under it. She exposed as much of her body as the law would allow. Her cigarette must have been four inches long. That was only one row, nine people.

There were more than 100, just sitting there, waiting for the plane to lift us from one community and set us down in another. It was difficult for me to look at the group–or any group like that–and not wonder how Jesus would see them.

"They are like sheep without a shepherd," I imagined him saying, as he did say of just such a group long ago.

There I sat in the middle of them without any way to tell them of our shepherd. Of course, I could have stood up and called out in a loud voice, "Listen, I can tell you about a person who can forgive your sin and give you a complete life of peace and victory and eternal life." They would not have listened because they would have looked upon me as one who was deranged. What I realized more fully that day was that each of these must be reached by someone living in their community.

If that Boeing 727 had crashed, the afternoon edition of the newspaper would have been headlined "Jet Crash. 129 Die" I wonder how many were prepared for God's prepared place. I closed my eyes, visualized Jesus hanging on the cross. I saw this waiting planeload standing gazing at him and watched more than half walk away without receiving his love. I didn't recognize any of the faces around the cross. Really the only person who looked happy enough to be saved was the large black woman. Of course, looks and outward appearances do not always indicate a person's spiritual condition. But on this occasion I did not have an impression that Christ had many "temples" in the room. I wondered if anyone could recognize Christ in me.

The value of ACTION loomed large as I realized that for the most part each of these must be reached for Christ in his own community by a local church and a concerned Christian. America is filled with situations like this. Who is going to reach them? If people like you, the reader, do not extend a hand of love, no one will. God is waiting for us to make ourselves available. This nation can be reached for the Lord.

The nation that forgets God is in trouble. And America is in trouble spiritually, morally, and financially. Now it goes without saying that God is sovereign, and he can reach our nation any way he wants to, but as I study the Word of God, I find that God usually uses those who are available. God will not use a people who deny the Bible. But most of us are still a people of the Book.

We have some outstanding denominations in America through which the Lord is working, but since I am a Southern Baptist, let me use them as one illustration of what can be done if we decide to reach this nation—now. We Southern Baptists have 35,000 Sunday Schools which are in business every week reaching and teaching people. We presently have approximately 7,250,000 people enrolled in our Sunday Schools, the largest number ever enrolled for Bible study by any denomination. But what could these 35,000 churches do in reaching others? We have seen what individual churches can do.

The First Baptist Church in Atlanta, Georgia, enrolled 800 new people in a week of enrollment. Southern Baptists have several hundred large churches like this one. What if half to three quarters of these churches did the same? What if all of our larger churches did the same? The Parker Memorial Baptist Church of Anniston. Alabama, had 650 in attendance on the Sunday it launched its enrollment week. During the week 233 new people were enrolled, and the following Sunday attendance gained 153 to reach 853. What would happen if even half our churches of this approximate size did the same as this church? Think of the lost people brought under the influence of Bible teaching and gospel proclamation. The New Hope Baptist Church of Palmetto, Florida, had 210 enrolled in Bible study and were averaging 130 in attendance at the time the church went into its ACTION enrollment week. The week saw 390 more people enrolled; enrollment jumped to 500. The attendance level rose to 290 and a high attendance day saw 324 present. We have several thousand churches the size of this one.

Can you even compute the results if large numbers of these churches went into ACTION and achieved similar results?

Austintown Baptist Church of Youngstown, Ohio, had 120 present on the Sunday morning their ACTION week began. Before Wednesday evening this church had enrolled eighty new people. What would this mean to every church with approximately 100 and less than 150 presently in attendance?

And what of the small, really small, church? Of our 35,000 churches, 20,000 have less than 100 present in Sunday School week by week. Many, if not most of these, are located in rural communities where population is small and attendance is somewhat limited. Matlacha Baptist Church of Pine Island, Florida, is such a church. Rather it *was* such a church before ACTION. The enrollment of this church was fifty, but during the ACTION week 170 new people were enrolled bringing enrollment to 220. If our 20,000 small churches would all enter into ACTION and achieve results anywhere approaching these, the results would be fantastic.

What would happen if every Southern Baptist pastor did the best he could to enroll new people. Could he enroll one new person each week? Could he enroll one new person each day? Every pastor could come somewhere within these two figures. Some could do even more.

All these figures together would add into millions. What would happen if an additional 5,000,000, 10,000,000, 15,000,000 people in America were enrolled in Bible study and began attending a Sunday School week by week. Think of the multiplied thousands whose lives would be changed as they moved from a study of God's Word to a personal knowledge of the Eternal Word, even Jesus Christ the Savior.

More churches have been established through Sunday Schools than in any other way. More people have been reached for salvation through Sunday Schools than in any other way. More people have been taught the Bible in Sunday Schools than in any other way. More people have been discipled for Christ through Sunday Schools than in any other way. Therefore, I challenge you to lead your church to do the following things.

(1) Use the ACTION Sunday School enrollment plan. The Baptist Sunday School Board of the Southern Baptist Convention has adopted ACTION as the official Sunday School enrollment program of the denomination. In the last few months it has revolutionized hundreds of churches where it has been used. Churches of several other denominations have used it successfully. Many churches have doubled, tripled, and even quadrupled in size within a year. This has produced revivals, growth, and evangelism unparalleled in almost all of them.

As developer of this mass-enrollment program, I hasten to say that nothing in the book is just theory. It has been beaten out on the anvil of experience. Churches of all sizes and location have experienced great growth.

(2) Challenge its leaders to enroll personally as many people as they can. Each one can set a goal to enroll fifty, seventy-five, 100, 125, or more during the next twelve

months.

(3) Establish at least one new Sunday School. Many churches can locate a nearby area where a new Sunday School is needed. Churches may also be able to sponsor a new Sunday School in an area distant from their own location. Literally thousands of areas have no Sunday School.

We can do anything we want to do, and I challenge you, one and all, to make this year your year to serve Christ with your maximum. I am only one voice, but as one voice I cry to my fellow Christians, "Let's win the multitudes to the Lord Jesus. Let's do it now."